# FACING

# OUR

# FUTURE

## BUILDING STRONG BLACK MEN
## IN THE TWENTY-FIRST CENTURY

JEREMIAH HOPES AND ZACK REYNOLDS Jr.

First Printing, 2015

10 9 8 7 6 5 4 3 2 1
ISBN-10: 0-9861405-0-3
ISBN-13: 978-0-9861405-0-1

Real Models Publishing
541 10th Street NW
Atlanta, GA 30318

Book design by Scarlett Rugers Design www.scarlettrugers.com

Ordering Information: Quantity sales. Special discounts are available on quantity purchases by corporations, associations, and others. For details, contact the publisher at the address above. Orders by U.S. trade bookstores and wholesalers, please contact us at info@facingourfuture.com.
Printed in the United States of America

# FACING OUR FUTURE

Jeremiah Hopes and Zack Reynolds Jr.

# CONTENTS

# Foreword

## Fulfilling the Vision for Black Men

Envision how the United States would look if all black men were reaching their full potential in all sectors of society. Let your imagination take you to a place that allows you to see how our communities can thrive. Think about how families and youth would thrive. Consider the economic impact and how the global competitiveness of this great country would be enhanced. Imagine how vastly different the public perception surrounding black men would be. This vision can become a reality if we encourage and support black men to take their rightful place in our society.

This book, *Facing Our Future: Building Strong Black Men in the Twenty-First Century* provides black men with a practical roadmap; the words in this volume are filled with passion and communicate a hope that will point us in the right direction. Throughout history, certain books are needed to propel a generation to a new level; this book fits that description. This is why I applaud the authors on their dedication to making a difference in society.

It is a common belief that if you take time to write a book, you must have something of value to add to society. In my review of this excellent book, the authors are providing something that is essential to all black men. The content will reach the depths of the souls of black men—who were put in this world for a divine purpose. I highly encourage every black man and everyone concerned about the plight of black men to purchase this book and fully engage with it. After engaging, I would encourage you to develop a plan of action to rebuild our community.

In closing, black men in our society are at a critical crossroads. Some have reached great measures of success, and others have underachieved. However, it is never too late to turn things in a positive direction. I can clearly envision a day when black men will reach all of the potential that was so masterfully placed in the depths of their souls. I look forward to the day that everything in this book will become a reality. However, it is up to each one of us that has an encounter with this book to do our part to make a difference. Enjoy this book and fully grasp the passion. Then understand this final directive: action is required!

Chance W. Lewis, PhD
Carol Grotnes Belk Distinguished Professor of Urban Education College of Education
The University of North Carolina at Charlotte
http://www.chancewlewis.com
http://www.thecollaborative.uncc.edu

*"You are either part of the solution or part of the problem."*
*- Leroy Eldridge Cleaver*

# A Note To Our Readers

We believe transparency is needed in order to provide the guidance, hope, and encouragement to build strong black men. Throughout this book we have included personal stories and commentary from our individual perspectives: Jeremiah writes as a mental health professional, and as a son reared in a single-parent, mother-led home and Zack's as a professional educator, mentor, and son reared in a two-parent, father-led home. We hope that you will be inspired by our experiences as we all collectively work to build and support strong black men.

The topic of building strong black men is comprehensive and one book cannot address the whole of this immense subject. However, this book is designed to engage in a discussion that must continue and grow into action. Please read this work with a desire to act. Refuse to be a part of the problem by complaining and blaming. Decide to be a part of the solution by taking action and doing your part to build black boys into strong black men.

# Introduction

Are you passionate about the success of young black men? Have you grown tired of all the negative imagery depicting black men as intimidating, unproductive thugs with no vision or hope for the future? Are you weary of the countless stories of young black men dying at the hands of those who place no value on their lives? What can be done to address and fill the gaps in the lives of young black men created by absent fathers? Do you have every intention of being part of the solutions-focused movement aimed at building up our young men? The fact that you're reading this book is proof that you do.

Throughout history black men have achieved greatness in all areas of human advancement. Black men have shown prowess in the areas of science, technology, business, and financial literacy. It is no coincidence that as our nation is currently lead by Barack Obama, the first black President of the United States of America, many young black men are gaining interest and becoming highly influential in the political arena. However, despite the great achievements of black men, the twenty-first century also offers great challenges.

We are entering an era where black boys are treated with fear and contempt, and their misbehavior and mistakes are met by undue and unmerited violence and aggression. Since we began writing this book, the deaths of Trayvon Martin, Michael Brown, and Jordan Davis took the national spotlight. However, they only represent three of the more than 10,890 black males who were murdered since 2012 according to the most recent data from the Federal Bureau of Investigation. Even if George Zimmerman and Officer Darren Wilson were convicted, their convictions would not have brought these young men back to their loved ones.

Black boys need guidance now more than ever. Black boys need mentors, fathers and father figures, high quality education, a proper understanding of what it means to be a man and how to treat the opposite sex. They need to understand that there is more to life than blazing a mic or bouncing a pass. Black boys are in need of answers to some of the tough questions they face in the twenty-first century. As men, mentors, counselors, educators, fathers, uncles, and leaders we must face them because they are our future. In a day and time where so much of the commentary about black men in the media is negative, we collectively decided to write a book as a positive tool to build and sustain strong black men.

In the pages that follow, you will learn how to:
- Help young black boys develop a proper perspective toward manhood.
- Begin the mentoring process.
- Assist boys in viewing members of the opposite sex with respect.
- See black boys as brilliant, not broken and beyond repair.

In each chapter you will find personal stories from our experiences as black men, as professionals who work directly with black boys, and as husbands and fathers. You will also find solutions-focused thinking to various concerns and challenges that are hindering the progress of black boys. Each chapter will also offer specific actions you can take to help build strong black men. Finally, each chapter ends with questions for the reader to answer as they seek to take action in their own spheres of influence.

As you read, we encourage you to fully engage and personalize your copy of this work with ideas and strategies that you and the stakeholders within your local community can implement practically and persistently. Thank you for your commitment and dedication! Now let's discuss how we can face the future head on and build strong black men.

# PART I

**MAN-YOU-FACTURING MEN**

**It's Called MENtoring For A Reason**

**The Man Of The House**

# 1
# MAN-YOU-FACTURING MEN

*"It is easier to build strong children than to repair broken men."*
*- Frederick Douglas*

Manhood is one of the most celebrated topics in our society. It attracts great debate and provocative discussions; yet its essence seems to escape us. A definition of manhood is elusive, and manhood is popularized in phrases such as "be a man," "man up," "a real man," or "a man's man." Our definitions of a "real man" vary, but we know that he is something to aspire to become. However, we often struggle to find men that we want our boys to emulate. If there is no real man in the home, this complicates the problem further.

Our culture has high expectations for manhood. If you are an adult male but lack certain qualities, such as integrity, a work ethic, trustworthiness, or respectfulness, we question whether or not you are a real man.

> It is not good enough to say "man up" or "be a man"; we must show them how.

There is something special, and even sacred, about becoming and being a man. It's something to be desired, anticipated, and bestowed. Manhood is not an ideal that can be packaged and then delivered. It cannot be reduced to age, height, weight, or income. Our society has created some very real distortions of the meaning and essence of manhood.

The sad reality is that many black boys are growing up without guidance and have models of manhood that are misrepresentations of what it means to be a man.

Black men must provide examples of manhood that reveal the essence of what it means to be a man and to live a life worthy of the title. Black boys need to see the images of real manhood, and we who are striving to uphold the standard of what it means to be a man must show them. It is not good enough to say, "man up" or "be a man"; we must show them how.

We are inclined to believe what we see. In order to reach young black men and help them to understand and properly define manhood, we must first be aware of the imagery they are receiving on a daily basis. We live in a world that often defines manhood by unrealistic criteria. A lot of time, money, and effort are put into the media's overwhelming imagery, which suggests that a *real* man:

- Does not cry or show emotion (other than anger)
- Can handle more than one woman at a time
- Is athletic
- Places no value on education or morals
- Is rich

How do we help our young men understand that a young woman is not something to be conquered? How do we help them resist the temptation of the fast money that drug trafficking promises? How do we help them understand the value of education and the necessity of commitment to a long-term vision that's bigger than *me, myself, and I?* The answers to these questions are not as elusive as they may seem. The answer lies within the *"we"*. We—as in all of us collectively—must take the time to demonstrate to them the true definitions of manhood. Let's explore some of the solutions we can implement.

***What do we need to teach them about how to treat the opposite sex?*** We must teach our young men that women are to be valued and respected. They are not merely objects created for male pleasure, games to be played, or servants with no purpose other than that of fulfilling male requests. Women possess intuition, a natural inclination to nurture, and an ability to communicate and sympathize. Therefore, we should teach our young men that a real man values both the emotional and the social intelligence of the women in their lives. They should treat all members of the opposite sex with the same respect and honor that they show their mother or sister.

***What do we need to teach them about resisting the temptation of the fast money that drug trafficking promises?*** We must show them the realities of the life of the typical drug dealer. Most are not rich and will inevitably spend valuable months and even years of their lives behind bars. If and when they are released, they leave the penal system with a prison record that can make it difficult to secure gainful employment, even if they have vowed to turn over a new leaf and abandon the drug trade. We must stress the advantages of living a life free from the fear of being busted or killed. We must also help them to understand that the customers that they sell to are being destroyed with every successful drug transaction they complete.

*What do we need to teach them about the value of education and the necessity of commitment to a long-term vision that's bigger than me, myself, and I?* If education doesn't appear to be important to us, it will not be important to them. Why should we expect them to care about their academics if we don't bother to check their assignments and homework, don't look at their report cards, and avoid parent-teacher conferences like the plague? We must make the time to communicate the importance of education and of having a plan for living a life of significance.

Influencing males to become lifelong learners must begin in the formative years (no later than elementary school) and involve being active in their academic life. Our level of engagement is directly connected to theirs. We must begin to define manhood to our young men by using these criteria for a real man:

- He is faithful and loves the woman that he is with
- He does what he says he is going to do (he has integrity)
- He takes responsibility for his actions
- He does not demand respect, but *earns* it
- Knows his greatest strength is not physical, but intellectual

Manhood is far too important for us to allow negative and distorted images to resound as the loudest messages our young men hear and see. If we are going to build our boys into strong black men, they must see a balanced view of black men, and other black men must lead the way in showing them what it really means to "man up."

## Manhood Begins When Childhood Ends

For boys, manhood begins when childhood ends. Many cultures perform rites of passage to confirm a boy's graduation to manhood. This serves as a public display both to the boy who is coming of age and to the village or community that he belongs to. At a certain point in a boy's life, he should stop doing things associated with childhood. There is nothing wrong with leisure, but we fail our young men when we continuously allow them to behave as children when they should be assuming responsibilities related to manhood.

| A boy's mentality . . . | A man's mentality . . . |
| --- | --- |
| *Thinks money grows on trees* | *Works to generate revenue* |
| *Talks too much* | *Listens twice as much as he speaks* |
| *Focuses on how much he can take* | *Focuses on how much he can give* |
| *Complains and make excuses* | *Works and provides solutions* |

To help boys develop a willingness to assume the responsibilities of manhood we should AIM:

- *Assign* them mandatory responsibilities and sufficient opportunities to help out around the house.
- *Initiate* healthy conversations about masculinity to foster male pride. No male-bashing in their presence!
- *Mentor*—Black boys need to be mentored by strong black men. (See chapter 2 for more detail.)

## Lessons on Manhood Should Come from a Man

The best way for any young man to learn how to be a man is from another man. A young man's best example is a wiser, more experienced man that he can relate to. We don't necessarily mean older as in senior citizen; we mean a male that is older than he is or that he can look up to.

It is critical that black males receive lessons on manhood from black males. Strong black men know the issues, challenges, and obstacles that these young men will face time and time again. They are equipped to provide them with firsthand testimonies that will allow them to be better prepared when life starts to throw curveballs and punches of disappointment.

We have a tremendous amount of respect for all women, both black and of other ethnicities that rear young black men on their own. Life presents many scenarios that require us to simply do what we've got to do. The reality is that many women, out of necessity, are "manning up" by doing the jobs of absent fathers and men. It's time for black men to step up! If we are not there, someone will step in and do the job we were created to do. We can no longer wash our hands of the dilemma facing young black men with phrases such as "That's not *my* son," "*Somebody* needs to talk to that young man," and "If he was *mine*, I would ..." Men that grew up fatherless must not be bitter and therefore ignore these young men so that they too have to figure it out alone. When we are completely honest, we know that none of us actually figured it out on our own either.

In many interviews with young black men, we've learned that they consider *real men* to be the ones who take a personal interest in them and actively look out for their well-being. This is why the lure of the drug dealer or gang leader is so attractive; it is a pathway to validation and stability. Starting with the early years, instructions on how to aim in the toilet, how to deliver a confident handshake, how to make eye contact when speaking or listening, and how to ask a girl out on

> *It is critical that black males receive lessons on manhood from black males.*

a date are all lessons boys should receive from men. Receiving these instructions from men establishes the self-confidence and provides the validation and sense of security that many young men are lacking. We can assure you in advance that the young women who will one day grow up to be the girlfriends and eventually wives of these young men will greatly appreciate it!

## Mother-Led Homes

Ideally, fathers should be present to raise boys into men, but many black boys are being raised by women without the help of a father. Given the abundance of single mother-led homes, how can boys learn the essentials of manhood? No two situations are identical, and everyone is different, but here are a few patterns that we have seen in the lives of single mothers who have and who are raising strong black men.

1. *They don't make excuses for their sons when they need correction.* These mothers have faced the fact that, for whatever reason, the father is not present, and they embrace the fact that fatherlessness does not mean their sons have to fail. Instead of blaming the absent father and excusing their sons' behavior, they work to find productive ways to help their sons overcome their challenges.
2. *They refrain from making their sons their companions and confidants.* Their sons always remain sons. These mothers make sure they have places and people to turn to when they need to vent or blow off steam. They take care of themselves so they can take care of their sons. They do not confide adult-oriented information to their sons or expect them to be the men in their lives.
3. *They understand their limitations and work to expose their sons to positive male figures.* Sometimes uncles, coaches, and mentors help provide the male perspective that they lack. These moms are secure enough to know that they are still the most important teacher and example, but they also know that positive men can enhance the work they are doing.
4. *They gradually give their sons age-appropriate responsibilities.* Taking out the trash, carrying groceries, washing dishes, and mowing the lawn may seem insignificant, but they provide a transition period for a boy in his quest for manhood. Giving him responsibilities allows him to gradually build his

confidence and test his strength (for example, "How many grocery bags can I carry?"). It also provides him with tangible ways that he can help his mother. These responsibilities help him to see that as he grows, more and more is expected of him.

5. ***They prepare their sons to face the fact that they are black males in a world full of challenges for the black male.*** Single mothers raising black boys naturally want to protect their sons from racism, stereotyping, and negative media portrayals, but they recognize that their sons are likely to encounter all of the aforementioned challenges. Even in twenty-first century America, it is likely that young black males will experience racism no matter how they wear their hair, what university they attend, how much money they make, or how successful they become. Racism and stereotyping are much less overt than they once were, but they still exist and extend across economic, educational, and social lines. Mothers play an important role in teaching their sons that they do not have to fit into a stereotypical mold. They are unique and possess a capacity for far more than the limitations presented by negative and often ill-advised stereotyping.

## Tough Love

Multiple definitions exist for the concept of tough love, but an excellent depiction of it is shown in the movie *Ray*, the remarkable story of Ray Charles, played by Jamie Foxx. Not only did Charles have to overcome the overt racism and prejudice of his era, he also had to overcome physical blindness. It would have been easy for his mother to make every excuse for why he could not succeed, but instead she loved him enough to prepare him for the harsh realities that would greet him in the future. The words spoken by his mother in an opening scene fit the description of tough love. They may sound harsh, but the intent is full of love.

> *I ain't gonna beat around the bush with you. You going blind. The doctors say ain't nothing they can do, so we gotta do it ourselves. [Ray starts to cry.] Stop it, stop it right now; we ain't got no time for no tears! Ain't nobody gonna have no pity on you just because you going blind. Now wipe them eyes. Okay, I'll show you how to do something once. I'll help you if you mess up twice, but the third time you on your own. Because that's the way it is in the world.* [1]

A number of scenes later, we see that Ray falls down in the house, and he begs and screams for his mother's help. Though she is only a few feet away, she remains quiet; she says nothing and does nothing. Against her instincts, she refrains from helping him. When he realizes that he is "on his own," he picks himself up and

1 Taylor Hackford, Director, *Ray*, 2004

uses his senses to help orient himself to his surroundings. His sense of hearing becomes keener, and he hears things that he had overlooked before.

In that defining moment, Ray became a man. Of course he did not physically transform into a man, but he had grasped the lesson his mother was trying to teach him. He learned that he had to pick himself up and use all his resources to his advantage. Yes, as his mother said, he was blind, but he was not stupid.

In the twenty-first century, young black boys face hurdles and obstacles that could impede their progress, but like Ray's mother, single mothers in particular have the honor of speaking life into their sons. Your son may not be blind, but you can speak to the many other obstacles in his way. You don't have to use the same tone as Ray's mother, but you do have to speak into his life and tell him he is not whatever a racist and stereotyping society may say he is.

## From Boys to Men

In many cultures, manhood is not just stumbled upon due to taking classes in the school of hard knocks. Many men have told us that their journey to manhood was built on a lifetime of mistakes and poor decisions; but the road to manhood doesn't have to be paved with mistakes. In the Jewish culture, for example, when a boy turns thirteen, he is considered to be accountable for his actions and thus subject to the law. He is called a *bar mitzvah*, which is translated "son of the law or commandment." He is often celebrated and given great honor. With the honor comes the responsibility to uphold the law and to take an active role in religious ceremonies. At thirteen, a son of the law understands that he has specific expectations and obligations to meet. [2]

In traditional African societies, rites of passage were a systematic process that began at birth and continued throughout the life cycle. There were five basic initiation rites that guided the growth and development of children in many African societies:  the rite of birth, the rite of adulthood, the rite of marriage, the rite of eldership, and the rite of ancestorship. Each community performed its own unique expression of each of the five rites. The adulthood or manhood rites for boys were initiated at the age of twelve or thirteen. They often included some type of seclusion from their families so that they could learn the essentials of manhood and the expectations for membership in that community. The specific procedures varied from group to group but all emphasized the passage process. [3]

It is interesting that in both Jewish and African cultures, manhood celebrations and expectations begin at puberty. One explanation for this is that the bodies of

2 Simon J. Bronner, "Fathers and Sons:  Rethinking the Bar Mitzvah as an American Rite of Passage," Children's Folklore Review 31 (2008-2009): 7-34.
3 Ampim, Manu. The Five Major African Initiation Rites. Africana  Studies. http://www.manuampim.com/AfricanInitiationRites.htm (Retrieved June 4, 2012).

young men can physically reproduce at that time, so it is important that they learn to be responsible with their newly acquired reproductive prowess. Reproductive ability comes with age, but productive ability comes with training and experience. You are not a man just because you can reproduce; you are a man when you can produce. The work of a man is not in the planting of seed, but rather in the watering, nurturing, and development of their seed. A farmer that merely plants his seed and abandons his crop leaves it vulnerable to noxious weeds, malicious pests, and stray animals that devour the plants, resulting in a pitiful harvest. In other words, the farmer's negligence toward his seed ultimately leads to his own demise.

For black boys in the United States, it is crucial that we place a consistent emphasis on rites of passage. These do not have to mirror rites of other cultures, but they have to be done. They must happen because young men, especially at the age of twelve or thirteen, are experiencing many changes. A rites-of-passage process helps them understand that they are growing up and that with that growing up comes certain responsibilities they have to meet.

Many young men that I have treated in the juvenile justice system begin their path to delinquency by the age of twelve. One of my most telling discoveries occurred early in my career with a simple survey of a group of young men. They were referred to me for various behavioral, emotional, and substance abuse concerns. The survey asked each young man to report anonymously his age when he first engaged in the following behaviors or acts:

- Shot a gun
- Used drugs
- Had his first kiss
- Had sex
- Sold drugs
- Drove a car

The average for each young man was twelve years of age. By the time he began treatment, each young man had a criminal record consisting of charges such as larceny of motor vehicles, gun and drug possession, and breaking and entering. The young men in the treatment program all had severe and exceptional behavioral and emotional disorders. By no means are we suggesting that *all* young black males are engaging in these behaviors, and much less at such a young age. But we are saying that twelve and thirteen are pivotal ages for all young men.

*The work of a man is not in the planting of seed, but rather in the watering, nurturing, and development of their seed.*

If a young man can shoot a gun, have sex, use drugs, and so on at twelve, why can't he learn that he has responsibilities as he grows and matures? Young men in the juvenile justice system adopt destructive behavior patterns because they are learning about manhood from gang leaders, drug dealers, and other peers who have developed their own rites of passage. Young men have reported to me that they felt powerful when they shot a gun, robbed someone, made their own money by selling drugs, or were accepted as a valued member of a gang. In fact, street gangs have elaborate initiation rites that prospective members have to endure to gain acceptance. If law-abiding and responsible men are not present to provide validation, our boys will find alternate routes for satisfying this essential craving deep in their hearts and psyches.

Again, we can provide for our young men a rites-of-passage process. A colleague once shared a story that could serve as an example of a rites-of-passage ceremony contextualized for the twenty-first century. In this case, the young man was around late adolescence. He was taken to a heavily wooded trail by a male family member and was told to walk down a path through the woods. His only instruction was to walk. It was well after sunset, and there were no streetlights to illuminate his path—just darkness and the night air.

As he walked, a presence came from behind and walked next to him. He did not know who it was; he only heard his voice. The voice was familiar. It may have been an uncle or another family member, but the voice talked to him about how he had seen him mature into a man and about the challenges ahead, not only on that dark path, but on the path of life as well. After a few minutes, the man stopped walking, and the young man continued.

As he walked a little further, another presence came from behind him. This time it was another man who had an influence in his life. This man, similar to the first, spoke to him about how proud he was of the young man's growth and development. He talked to him about how he had overcome challenges and had come away stronger. After a few minutes, this man too faded back into the darkness.

As he continued, man after man approached this adolescent, who was on the brink of a transition. Each man, whether an uncle, coach, teacher, or family friend, spoke words of encouragement, pride, and affirmation into his life. Finally, at the end of the trail, a lone man standing in tears greeted him. The man was his father, who was the last to give his blessing and assurance that this adolescent boy was now a man.

You can imagine the pride and confidence the young man must have felt as he walked down that dark path. Of course, his walk down that path was symbolic of how these men had been with him as he journeyed down the path of life. After such an affirming ritual, the young man must have felt confident in his manhood. If he'd had any doubts, they were dispelled that night.

> *If law-abiding and responsible men are not present to provide validation, our boys will find alternate routes for satisfying this essential craving deep in their hearts and psyches.*

At school the next week, he must have walked a little taller and showed more confidence. Even if a peer in his school had called him a punk, a lame, or any other derogatory name, he would likely have just smiled at the accuser and stood tall in his newly affirmed manhood. There is no need for a man to fight a boy over childish words.

Often boys who strive to prove their manhood by trumping themselves through fighting, bullying, selling drugs, or other illegal acts have not been affirmed in their manhood. They are insecure, and because they doubt their own legitimacy, they find themselves going to great and often extreme measures to convince themselves of something that should have been bestowed upon them by strong and loving men through a rites-of-passage process.

We have much to learn from the traditions of other cultural groups, but we have to develop our own specific practices. If we, as concerned and responsible men, do not initiate our boys into manhood, we leave them vulnerable to the gang leaders and drug dealers who, unlike us, *have* developed a system and a process of initiation into their culture, even though it ultimately fails to usher them to manhood. It only escorts them to the criminal lifestyle, prison, and sometimes death.

*The quality of our choices is directly connected to the level of our character.*

Manhood has to be modeled, because boys will do what they see us do. Establishing a rites-of-passage process in your home, school, church, or community is essential for helping transition boys into men. To do this, gather a group of men who are interested in building boys into men. Together plan a series of events that will take place at certain times, such as just before the beginning of a new school year, during the summer, before a birthday, at graduation into the next grade level, or any other significant times in a boy's life.

A rites-of-passage process does not have to be elaborate. However, it does have to be intentional, consistent, and clear each time a boy passes into a new stage in his life. For example, the weekend before my son turned four, we spent the weekend together. I was intentional about how we spent our time. We went to the store and bought a tent, set it up in the living room, and watched a father-son cartoon on his level. I let him choose the tent, and he helped me assemble it, which gave me the opportunity to instruct and encourage him along the way.

During breakfast the next morning, I briefly explained that he was turning four and talked about what that meant, such as starting preschool, being away from home during the day, meeting new friends, and learning new activities. I told him that I was proud of him and that I loved him.

This is an example of something that you can do with your son, nephew, grandson, cousin, or mentee. Make it specific to the young men or young man you are working with.

## Character 101

The essence of a man is not how physically strong or attractive he is. Manhood should not be defined by how loud you can yell, how much bass is in your voice, or whether you can hold back tears when experiencing pain. In his "I Have a

Dream" speech, the iconic Reverend Dr. Martin Luther King Jr. stated he desired that his children be judged "by the content of their character." The character of a man is who he really is at his core. It's what he does when no one is watching. It's also what others remember about him long after his physical presence leaves the room. When discussing manhood with young black men, we must communicate the importance of strong character.

I have certainly taught my share of state-regulated curriculum in the public education system, but there is not much curriculum on how to make wise choices. You won't find character education in the educational standards required by most states in our nation; it's considered optional. Ironically, character education is probably the most valuable form of schooling we will ever receive. For example, you can have tons of educational credentials and degrees, but if you choose to live a life of crime, you may end up spending significant time, if not the rest of your life, behind bars.

A *man's man* is dependable, respectful of others, and professional. As men, it is essential to rediscover our ability to keep promises and follow through with commitments. The quality of our choices is directly connected to the level of our character. Whether our young black men make good or bad choices, we must remind them that they will have to live with the consequences.

## The Essentials of Manhood

Below are a few essentials that we believe are important for young black men to internalize as they attempt to develop an understanding of what manhood really means.

***Manhood is knowing when to fight.*** Men choose their battles wisely. When a man walks away from a physical or verbal fight, he understands why he is choosing to walk away. Walking away is not a sign of weakness or even fear but rather a sign of maturity and self-control—both of which are essential qualities of manhood. Men fight only when they have to. There is no need to fight just to prove they are men; *real men* know that fighting just to fight proves very little.

Many young men in my counseling practice have a history of violence. They have witnessed intense violence, perpetrated it, and been victims of it themselves. Fighting and other aggressive behaviors have become a natural form of expression. Therefore, resistance is understandable when they begin counseling for anger management; I understand when I meet resistance from them when we work on managing their anger and on de-escalating violence. When we discuss the importance of being able to walk away from a physical fight, it seems like a form of weakness to them. They often ask something like, "So you want me to just *walk away* if someone hits me? If I do that, everyone will think I'm weak."

Is there ever a time to use physical force? There is a time and place for everything, and a great mark of manhood is the ability to discern the time and place. You fight when your life is in danger or the life of a loved one or someone who is unable to defend themself is in danger. Physical fighting is a last resort; it is for when there is no other solution. We live in an era when fistfights are legends because now guns and other weapons are used, and the showdowns often end with fatalities.

It is important for young men to learn that finding solutions to their problems without turning to violence is a great mark of manhood that is much more difficult than throwing a few blows or pulling a trigger. If we are going to succeed at raising strong black men, we have to model for them the essential quality of strength of character without resorting to physical violence. We have to be intentional about this approach, because they are bombarded with messages that tell them to do otherwise.

A great way to help boys manage conflict successfully is to emphasize the importance of timing and self-control. It is common for boys to act on impulse, but if we are going to help build them into strong men, we must point out these facts:

- There is a time to shoot the ball and a time to pass.
- There is a time to speak and a time to listen.
- There is a time to laugh and a time to cry.
- There is a time to work and a time to play.

Knowing how to determine the appropriate time and place can be one of the most valuable skills we teach. It can benefit them in many different situations: in school, in sports, in the home, and in the community.

***Manhood is confidence, not arrogance.*** There is very little that communicates confidence better than being aware of your identity and having made peace with how you were made. Men accept both the best and the worst of themselves. They seek ways to enhance their weaknesses and build their strengths. They know that they do not have it all together, and they have no need to pretend that they do. They are honest with themselves and others. They come clean and admit when they are wrong, and they work to learn from their mistakes. Arrogance is based on insecurity and deception. The arrogant person has weaknesses but cannot own those weaknesses. He inflates his strengths and minimizes—or even denies—his weakness.

> *There is a time and place for everything, and a great mark of manhood is the ability to discern the time and place.*

***Manhood is leadership.*** A man should add value to the people that surround him. Your family and friends should be better people because of you. Your school or sports team should be better because of you. A man should recognize inner strengths that will not only make him successful, but will make others around him better as well. This is a part of leadership, and learning to lead is a part of becoming a man.

*Manhood is developing and maintaining a proper attitude and perspective toward women.* We should teach young men that a real man values both the emotional and the social intelligence of the women in their lives. Whether it is their mother, sister, girlfriend, etc., we must encourage them to listen to women attentively. They need to listen twice as much as they speak, not simply so that they can get what they want, but so they develop an appreciation for the purpose and role of a woman in the life of a man. Teach them to view every woman as a valuable human being, reminding them that she is someone's daughter, sister, or mother.

*Manhood is about decisiveness and being both responsible and accountable to others for the decisions you make.* Every cause has an effect. Whether our young black men make good or bad choices, we must remind them that they will have to live with the consequences. We must encourage them to think soundly and judiciously before they speak and act. The choices we make are directly linked to our character and values. In our society, men are expected to lead, so they will be judged heavily by the decisions that they make.

*Manhood is synonymous with being a father, provider, nurturer, and protector.* Let's keep it real. Ask most women what they *expect* from their husband, the father of their children, or their future partner, and you are almost certain to hear references to these roles. If a man is not clear about his role, a woman will tell him! Why? Because women have to master womanhood. They are clear about what a woman is, so they can naturally communicate to our young men what men are *not*. This is precisely why we took the time to explore how the role of the female—particularly the single mother—is critical in the twenty-first century. We teach young black men that they will be expected to be active leaders in their families. We explain to them that men play a major role in the financial and emotional support of their families and will continue to do so in the twenty-first century. To communicate anything differently to young black men about what will be expected of them as they get older and start families is to fail them and lead them astray.

*Manhood is displaying intelligence, excellence, and morality.* We must teach our young men that intelligence (not poor scholastic performance), excellence (not mediocrity), and morality (not promiscuity and unethical behavior) are in fact *cool* as well as crucial to their ability to lead productive lives. The media often presents images of men being out of control, using impaired judgment, cheating on their spouses or significant others, and incapable of listening.

To succeed at building strong black men, we must equip them to walk in the confidence that comes along with putting their best self forward at all times. We must teach them how to dress for success, to speak with proper diction, and to read books and other literature that encourages them to think wholesome, productive thoughts about themselves and the world around them. We must emphasize being principled and remind them that they are too intelligent to fall for the skewed images that suggest men are irrational, ignorant of basic social and life skills, and unable to control their urges and emotions.

## What's in a Name?

I had the awesome privilege of discussing identity as it relates to young black males with three accomplished black women in a Starbucks during one of my many writing sessions. I asked them if they were mothers. With much enthusiasm they answered, "Yes!" These three women were responsible for six young black men ranging in age from five to eighteen. One of the women, the mother to an eighteen-year-old, sixteen-year-old, and an eleven-year old, spoke with great passion as she elaborated on the phrase "What's in a name?" The answer: *Everything*!

In this world, judgments and decisions are made every day based on the perceived value of names and brands. In some African cultures, a name has such great significance that a child is not named until days after his birth. The parents and elders want to have time to select a suitable name for the child. In some cases, certain events assist the family in naming him. For example, if he is born during a time of a plentiful crop, his name will reflect the blessings and abundance of the community. In the United States, names such as Colgate, Nabisco, Kellogg, Hewlett-Packard, Ford, and Rockefeller bring to mind specific imagery and expectations. There is no confusion or questions regarding the identity of these brands.

We must communicate to young black men the meaning and importance of a name. If we encounter a child whose name doesn't have a clear meaning, we should remind him of his significance and that there never was, nor ever will be, another individual just like him. Even identical twins have distinct fingerprints. We must *verbally* communicate that if they don't make their contribution to this world, it will *never* be made. Young black men should be validated at home, but if they are not receiving it at home, we must make time to pull them aside and validate them ourselves. "Sticks and stones may break my bones but words will never hurt me" is one of the biggest lies ever told! Words help and words hurt. Words are powerful. Words matter. Names are words. What's in a name? *Everything.*

One of the greatest personal tragedies is the confusion a human being experiences when he doesn't know his own identity. When you aren't sure of who you are, you will drift back and forth between the opinions of others in a constant state of confusion, accomplishing nothing. Many of our young black men are experiencing this. When they don't know who they are, it is easy for them to buy into an image of who they are supposed to be. They are likely to believe these images if they do not have a sense of identity. A strong black man knows how to dismiss images that are not consistent with his nature and character. Perfect the art of being yourself; be confident in that, and let the trends grow around you. If you do not know who you are, it is easy to allow other influences to define you. Remember: *you* define you.

> *When you aren't sure of who you are, you will drift back and forth between the opinions of others in a constant state of confusion, accomplishing nothing.*

## Hammers, Nails, and Quality Time

It was a major undertaking to say the least. "We've never done this before!" "It's summertime." "How long is this going to take again?" "What about a fishing trip, or a trip to Myrtle Beach, or playing a game of HORSE?" My excuses and reasons for not doing the project were plentiful. Just what type of project, you ask? My dad decided the summer—the last summer of my high school experience, while in the midst of AAU basketball, camps, and anything else that a teenage boy would want to do with his time off—would be the best time to build a storage facility. Not just any storage facility though. It was a sixteen-by-twenty, insulated, built-in garage and man cave of his—I mean *our*—dreams!

Now, at the time I thought this would be torture. First of all, carpentry was not the family business. As a matter of fact, our neighbor a mere two doors down the street was a full-fledged carpenter. He could do a project like that in his sleep. Second, we had never attempted anything like it before, so there was no previous experience, good or bad, to go by. So why bother? One thing was for sure: we were going to be spending a *lot* of time together. Not that I minded, as my father and I have always had a great relationship. He instilled in me the belief that I could do anything I set my mind to, apparently even things that I had no professional aspirations to do, like *carpentry*! But we are more similar than we are different. We both take pride not just in doing the right things, but in doing things right. Therein lay the problem. As a boy, my father taught me that a man should put forth his best effort at any task that he attempts. Some of my dad's favorite admonitions were:

*"Take pride in your work."*
*"Work until the job gets done."*
*"Don't cut corners."*
*"You can fix it now or you can fix it later, but you will have to fix it."*

So with this type of training I knew we wouldn't be starting the project to merely pour some messy concrete, halfheartedly tack up some sheetrock and plywood, or put up a garage door that would not function properly. We were going to do it right or not do it at all. Even if it took *all* summer.

We began by doing something that my father taught me and that I believe is important for any man, young or old, to understand: When you don't know something, don't be afraid or ashamed to ask questions. The male ego is often a man's worst enemy. Remember the carpenter neighbor I mentioned earlier? We invited him over to discuss our project and to receive his everything-you-need-to-know-before-you build-this-storage-facility list of carpentry dos and don'ts. Of course, he did these types of projects every day, so he knew exactly how and where to start. His description made it seem relatively easy, and he mentioned we'd probably be done before we knew it. "*Yes! Give me a hammer and some nails, and let's go to work!*" I thought. Well, not so fast. There was just this little bitty hurdle we had to clear: you can't build without building supplies. As motivated as we were, there would be no building without first purchasing the materials. This reminds me of another important manhood lesson I learned as a youngster: you must first count the cost before getting started in a new venture or project.

I feel that this is a great time to remind you that neither one of us was getting paid for this project. That's right. Not only were the two of us going to be working hard daily outside in the middle of a scorching North Carolina summer, but we were also going to be working for free. Now, sometimes working for free will actually cause you to get paid, but I'll get back to that concept a little later. So we went to the local home improvement stores and purchased the building supplies. Then we returned home and gathered the blueprint to begin working on the storage facility. Remember when I mentioned "doing it right or not doing it at all"? I knew that "doing it right" could take all summer. I would love to be able to tell you that we built everything perfectly from the ground up the first time, but of course that would be, well, a lie. The truth is that sometimes we got it right and sometimes we didn't. This is very important to understand. Take notes. First of all, I learned that in order to achieve a goal or to accomplish anything in life, you must first start. If you don't start, you'll never finish.

> *When you don't know something, don't be afraid or ashamed to ask questions.*

We are all human, and we don't have all the answers when we first begin a new project or task. As a man, you learn by making mistakes, and just like in everyday life, you learn to trust your instincts based on previous experiences. How do you know you are on to something? You will always know when you've done something good—or bad, for that matter—when people begin to take notice.

I have many fond memories of being raised in a small town. That kind of life allows you to have some great life experiences that you learn to appreciate more as you get older. One characteristic of most small towns, especially in the South, is that the people know each other. They actually take the time to stop and say hello. This is one of the reasons it took us longer than I expected to complete the building. Everyone from aunts and uncles to my friends' parents to random strangers began to stop by out of curiosity to ask what in the world we were doing. When they realized what we were doing, many of them asked how much we would charge to build a storage facility for *them*.

I mentioned earlier that working for free could cause you to get paid. We received an offer from an out-of-state visitor who saw the building near its completion to provide food, shelter, building supplies, and compensation if we would agree to build the exact same facility on his property. Let me remind you again that my father and I had absolutely *no* experience doing carpentry together before this project. This offer and the many people that simply dropped by just to say "hello" and "keep up the good work" were very inspiring and encouraged us to take even more pride in our work and to finish what we'd started. Our commitment to doing the job right had introduced us to the possibility of a new business venture.

It's been about twenty years since the building was completed, and just in case you're curious, *yes*, it's *still* standing. There was something that my father knew way back then that I would not understand until I purchased my first home. We were not only constructing a storage building as a father-and-son bonding activity, we were also completing a home improvement project. With every piece of wood that we nailed up or down, we were adding more value to our home. The building itself had value, and that particular value is now factored into the value of the entire property that my parents own.

Today I am extremely grateful that I was able to share that experience with my father. I will always cherish it. As fathers, mentors, and coaches of young black men, let us proactively create opportunities to teach, to bond, and share skills and experiences that add value, create lasting memories, and ultimately serve to build strong black men.

# Action Steps

*How can you cultivate rites of passage for the black boys in your sphere of influence?*

*How can you help black boys combat some of the misconceptions and distortions about manhood?*

*Discuss and develop a plan that is specific and realistic for you to implement.*

# 2
# It's Called MENtoring For A Reason

*Mentors build mentors. Leaders build leaders. When you look at it closely,*
*it's really one and the same thing.*
*- Tony Dungy*

Human beings were designed for relationships and social interaction. In our effort to help build strong black men, we cannot ignore the importance of mentoring and the role it plays in the lives of males, both youth and adults. The interesting thing about the need for relationships is that we practically refuse to go without them. For example, consider the boy aspiring to athletic greatness. He isn't patient enough to wait for that magical interpersonal moment in which he receives an autograph from his beloved sports hero. Years before they ever meet, the boy has already designated him as his role model. He has read all about the athlete, memorized his birth date and stats, emulated his trademark moves, worn his signature shoes, and donned the same jersey number in his honor. They are best friends, even though the role model hasn't yet been informed of the seriousness of their relationship. One day they finally meet, and the boy's private designation is declared publicly: "I am your biggest fan! You're my role model!" The star athlete is flattered, but has no idea just how much he means to his young follower. That boy eventually becomes a man and takes an alternative career path to professional athletics and superstardom. In adulthood, the Fortune 500 CEO or successful entrepreneur often replaces the star athlete admired during childhood.

Even if no one volunteers to be our role model, we secretly nominate and select the role models of our choice. Keith, a young musician with aspirations to be a professional drummer, had been spending a lot of time shadowing Tony, his band director. Tony was an older, accomplished musician and had decided to spend some extra time with Keith based on his musical potential. One day, Tony spotted

> *A mentor lives a life worth emulating and is willing to share his time with another.*

Keith talking with a group of his friends and decided to walk over and say hello. To Tony's surprise, Keith enthusiastically introduced him as his mentor and band director.

Though there was no structured mentor-mentee relationship, it dawned on Tony that he had earned the title of mentor simply because of the time and effort he'd put into learning about Keith's life and aspirations. This was the result of one of their first talks; afterward, Tony took the time to assess his protégé's responses to questions related to his personal and career goals. This initial conversation evolved into an informal routine of meeting to share relevant information and to provide accountability. There is a lesson to be learned from this story: the designation of mentor is not always based on part-time volunteerism or employment with a mentoring program run by a nonprofit organization. A mentor lives a life worth emulating and is willing to share his time with another.

## Why Not Me?

What are your reasons for not mentoring? No matter how insignificant you think it is, there is a young black male out there that can benefit from your story, your time, and your attention. Every one of us must begin to ask the question "If I was accused of being a positive mentor for at least one young black male, would there be enough evidence to convict me?" The truthful verdict for many potential black male mentors would be "not guilty." Mychal Wynn, author of *Empowering African-American Males: A Guide To Increasing Black Male Achievement,* shared the following insight on this critical topic:

> *"African-American males mentoring other African-American males is one of the critical strategies that is required. In fact, it may be the most important strategy in ensuring the successful development and maturation of young African-American males into a generation of men who will be loving fathers to their children, faithful husbands to their wives, and leaders for their community."*

Below are some of the barriers, many of them mental, which impede black males from mentoring:

- Interested in being mentored themselves
- Assuming they don't make enough money (some men equate having money as key to being a mentor)
- Time constraints
- Lack of motivation and knowledge about the benefits of mentoring black males

- Not comfortable dealing with the rebelliousness of black male youth
- Previous challenges with law enforcement (men who have been arrested or incarcerated)
- Lack of trust of programs funded by the government
- Belief that only white collar black men can be mentors
- Inadequate training and ongoing support
- Inability to find mentoring programs in local communities
- Assuming they would need to spend money on mentees[4]

Everyone has a story. Everyone. Young black men need us to tell our story. They are starving for it! A lot of black men would like to mentor but don't know where to start. We cannot afford to allow this to be a barrier to providing the young men of our communities with the consistent, positive guidance they need. Getting involved is easier than you might think. There are national organizations, such as Big Brothers Big Sisters and 100 Black Men of America that have local chapters in cities across the United States. Both are respected organizations with longstanding mentoring programs. Their program coordinators scratch their heads daily due to the staggering numbers of young black males on the waiting lists of their mentoring programs. These eager mentees far exceed the number of adult black males that have declared themselves willing and available to mentor.

You may be reading this and thinking, *I would get involved with Big Brothers Big Sisters or 100 Black Men of America's mentoring initiatives, but I live in an area where there are no chapters nearby.* This is no excuse. Ask yourself this: "Who are the black boys in my local area who could benefit from mentoring?" Once you identify the boys who need mentoring, create your own mentoring organization or group. Pull together a group of boys from your neighborhood, your church, group home, or the local YMCA or youth sports organizations. Go to the schools in your district and ask to meet with the principals or teachers to find out if you can volunteer to mentor boys in your school district. The solution is simply to abandon excuses and to start where you are.

## What Makes a Good Mentor?

*Remember, a friend is not the same thing as a mentor.*

It's not enough to simply be a mentor. You must strive to be an *effective* mentor. There must be a wisdom and experience gap between any mentor and mentee. You cannot teach a person something you don't know. As a mentor, your expertise, wisdom, and experience create the essential environment of respect and the opportunity for continual learning. It also gives the mentee something to aspire to. Remember, a

4 David Miller, Man Up, Recruiting and Retaining African American Male Mentors. Dare To Be King. http://daretobeking.net/ (Retrieved December 14, 2012).

friend is not the same thing as a mentor. A friendship can develop from a mentor-mentee relationship, but that is not the primary objective. Mentors should have the capacity to expand a young man's personal growth.

## The Five Musts of a Mentor

Though not exhaustive, the following are five criteria mentors should follow. As a mentor, you *must:*

1. ***Keep your promises***. If you say you are going to do something, *please* do it. Many of our young men have not even completed junior high school yet, but have already experienced a lifetime's worth of broken promises.
2. ***Invest time rather than spend time***. Mentoring is so much more than spending a few hours a week with a young man attending an athletic event, watching a movie, or going out to eat. Mentoring is not babysitting. If you are just a babysitter, you don't have to work at ways to improve your mentee's life. You just have to monitor him for a specific amount of time. But in order for him to grow and develop you have to *invest* time. You have to care enough for him to assess his potential, personality, strengths, weaknesses, emotional needs, and insecurities. Knowing and understanding these essentials allows the mentor to invest their time in ways that will be most beneficial to the present and future of the mentee.
3. ***Help them identify and operate in their strengths***. Black men, both young and old, are extremely gifted. In many cases, particularly with young men, their gifts are uncultivated. A true mentor is one that seeks to develop this potential and knows how to tap into a mentee's reservoir to draw out and cultivate his gifts.
4. ***Deal with your insecurities***. Many men secretly decide not to mentor because they fear being replaced or surpassed by their potential protégé. The truth is that effective mentoring ultimately produces another self-sufficient male capable of developing his own mentees. These mentees benefit from your time, wisdom, and experience, thus enabling them to accomplish more over time.
5. ***Know when to release***. As much as we would like for our mentor-mentee relationships to last a lifetime, the truth is they won't. There comes a time when your mentee either has reached the end of his tenure under your mentorship or simply needs to broaden his horizons. If you have an issue with your mentee not needing you anymore, please reread number 4 above. No one person has all the answers. A true leader actually wants a successor and is secure with the lessons he has taught and the rapport he has built over time with his mentee. Mentorship is about making an impact that will last a lifetime, helping your mentee maximize his potential, and raising up another mentor who will pay it forward and repeat the process with another.

## Closed Mouths Don't Get Fed

We've talked a lot about the great need for mentors for young black men. But let's put the shoe on the other foot for a moment and talk about the responsibilities of the mentee in the mentorship relationship. How does a hungry mentee secure a potential mentor? Here are some specific criteria for aspiring protégés to consider when first starting the process:

- *Know what type of mentor you are looking for.* If you don't know what you want, no one can help you get it. Find someone who is doing what you want to do. Inform him of your personal goals and clearly express your aspirations and desire to glean from and serve with him.
- *Be clear.* Inform your mentor about what you feel you need from the relationship in order to grow and develop. After informing your mentor of your goals, let him guide you based on his wisdom and experience. This is for the benefit of both parties. By being clear, both of you are positioned to produce and receive the best results from the interaction.
- *Decide how long you want the mentoring relationship to last.* Some things require only a few meetings. Others may require months or years of mentoring. *Note:* Mentorship often produces more than either party expects. Don't slam a door shut that is just beginning to open!
- *Do your homework.* Learn as much as you can about the potential mentor before you approach him. Also remember that although your ideal mentor may be good at what he does, he may not be good at mentoring others in how to do it.
- *Be willing to learn.* A mentee is one who wants to learn. If you already knew it all, there would be no need for a mentor. Take full advantage of the opportunity to glean from your mentor's wisdom. Always have your notepad and recorder handy.
- *Respect his time.* Time is your most valuable commodity. If you want the mentorship to continue, respect and protect the time that your mentor shares with you. If you can't be on time, *be early*!
- *Don't be overbearing.* Your eagerness and enthusiasm for mentoring could become a turnoff if not channeled properly. When you make a request or ask for assistance, give him time to respond. You never know what he may be developing on your behalf.

# "How Mentorship Changed My Life"
## by Christian Gray

*Like many young black men, I grew up in a single-parent home led by my mother. I love my mom dearly, and she is the most important woman in my life. However, I had an extremely hard time obeying her rules. I was disrespectful, noncompliant, and even put my hands on my mother on some occasions. My mother worked several jobs, which meant I was home alone the majority of the time. I was in school during the day and home alone late at night. I never once resented my mother for constantly working and providing, but I acted out while at school and was disobedient. I was very disruptive, disrespectful, and a frequent visitor to the principal's office. One thing that separated me from others who had behavior issues was my academic ability. I never faced problems academically; my issues were always behavioral. My behavior and disrespectful attitude at home transferred over to my actions during school. I had no structure in my life. Don't get me wrong! I am not blaming my mother, because I know she was doing the best she could to provide for us. I sought attention regularly and did not have much regard for how I received it.*

*My mother gave birth to me at age sixteen. With such a small age difference between us, I looked at her more as a friend than a mother. This caused many issues in regard to discipline, because I refused to listen. Though very young, I was already the man of the house. My mother was always working, and there was no father or even a male figure present. I had a mother who worked all day and night, then came home late and tried to be a mother. It was tough because I was so angry from her absence that I acted out. The truth is without my mother I would not be half the man I am today.*

*With constant fighting verbally and physically between us, she'd finally had enough. Looking for answers and a new path for me, she was forced to send me away. At the beginning of fifth grade, she sent me to live with my father. It was like living with a stranger. I hadn't known anything about him; I hadn't known where he lived or with whom he lived. I knew absolutely nothing. But I respected him, and like many males, I feared my father. When my mother sent me to live with him, I resented her. I felt abandoned, and as if she did not love me anymore. Looking back at it now, I understand the burden I was placing on her by my constant misbehavior; she did what she felt was appropriate.*

*My father was very strict, and his discipline tactics were very traditional. I had structure and order, but it did not matter. I continued to make good grades and to misbehave in school. The only difference was the way I was disciplined by each parent. I would fight my mother, but not once thought about disrespecting my father, because of the fear he put into me. I did not look at him as a father figure or a role model; he was a disciplinarian, simply someone I had to face when I was misbehaving. His form of discipline was "corporal punishment"—spanking. My behavior was terrible while in school, and every time he received a phone call from school or I had some type of behavioral issue, it was handled with a spanking. I was spanked weekly, fairly hard at times. I resented my father for this, as I felt he did nothing but discipline me. Yes, I agree, I did need discipline. However, at that particular time, I needed a different approach and a neutral party. This is where a mentor was needed.*

*After living with my father for two years, I was able to move back with my mother. I had convinced her that I was ready to live with her and constantly reassured her that my behavior was commendable. She did not like me living with my father or the way I was treated while living with him, so this made it much easier for me. When I finally moved back in with her, I bounced directly back onto the path I'd been on before. Misbehaving in and out of school, fighting with my mother, not following directions—it was the same song as before, but this time I was older, which made the punishments more serious.*

*I was in the eighth grade when my life began to change for the better. I was introduced to a mentor who happened to be my social studies teacher as well as my assistant basketball coach. On the surface, I simply looked at him as my teacher and coach. I never looked at him as a mentor. With distance and mistrust from my father, I never once looked at another man for answers. With time, my mentor and I began to form a relationship. He never overwhelmed me with questions in regards to my behavior or looked for answers.*

*During this time, I still was behaving poorly in the majority of my classes and at home. With time I began to trust my mentor, and I looked to him for answers and advice. He looked like me, he played the same sport as me, and I labeled him as someone who actually cared. As the year went on, I became closer and closer with my mentor. He led by example and guided me as needed. I did not need a male in my life to make up for my father's absence; I needed a male in my life to help me become a man. I needed a man to teach me how to tie my first tie, to talk to me about women, school, and sports, and to embrace me as a young man. My mother is the strongest and most determined woman I know, but as a young man, I wanted another male to share things with and receive advice from. My mentor was that guy for me; he lived by what he preached to me, which is why I respected him. Deep down inside, I knew he was reaching out to me because he honestly cared and wanted to make a difference in my life.*

*When I first started high school, my behavior was better while in school, but at home it was a similar story as before. I was not sure what was going to happen with our relationship, but he did not fail me. We continued to stay in touch. I called him whenever I needed to; it did not matter what the situation was. I liked having a male that I could rely on and trust. My mentor helped me become a man, and I give him credit for changing my life and getting me on the right path. He did not just talk to me about my issues and tell me everything was going to be all right. He became a part of my life; he wanted to make a difference and he did. When I was wrong, he stepped in and told me. He shared things with me that were important to him in his life. He was that man in my life that I'd never had.*

*A young man will accept direction and correction from a man once he knows he really cares about him. My mother was great, but there are certain things that a woman cannot give a young, troubled man. My mentor introduced me to his family; he made me set goals; he talked to me about being a better man, obeying my mother, continuing to be a good student, succeeding in life, and much more. He was positive but realistic at the same time. When I set goals to reach, he would make me develop a plan to reach those goals, which was important because it gave me structure.*

*Now that I'm an adult, my mentor and I still have a remarkably close relationship, and I can honestly say that building a relationship with my mentor was the best thing that has happened to me. He showed me what it was like to be a positive man; he has had a lifetime impact on me, and even those around me. Not only was he a mentor to me, he was a mentor through me. The positive information that he was sharing with me, I would share with my friends who were out in the streets, and it would give them insight into better things. I had friends creating goals for themselves, and I tried to help them get on the right path. Soon I began to lead just as my mentor had led me. My friends began to look to me for answers and follow in my footsteps as I walked down the right path.*

*Mentorship is a gift that keeps giving. I am currently a mentor to troubled youth who remind me of myself growing up, thinking they know everything and not wanting help from anyone. The difference now is that I can relate. I give young men hope, just as my mentor did for me. I believe this is the most significant step in life—having hope. When a person believes in himself or herself and has a supporting cast that does, it makes all the difference. A mentor is important in any individual's life. It does not matter what race, background, socioeconomic status, or side of town the individual comes from.*

*Everyone needs a mentor. A mentor is someone reliable, someone who listens as well as gives you advice. When all you see is struggle or pain, it is a blessing to have someone there for you who will respond, reassure you that you can make it, and give you that extra push when you need it. Everyone needs a push in life. It does not matter if you are filthy rich or dirt poor. Everyone needs a push, and the most beautiful thing about this is that when you are pushed, you then want to push others who are close to you, who mean something to you. Mentorship is a gift that keeps giving. Make the best of it.*

## Men Need Mentors Too

In our discussion of mentorship, we cannot assume that all men will extend themselves to become mentors. It is easy to become critical when we hear others lament the lack of black fathers, role models, and mentors. Given some of the more daunting realities facing many of our young black men it is tempting to ask, "Why aren't we doing more?" However, the need for mentors extends well beyond juveniles. Many black men, though they may not admit it, are still looking for their own father, role model, and mentor. As featured in the survey, *Man Up: Recruiting & Retaining African American Male Mentors*, the number-one reason for not mentoring reported by respondents was that *they* needed mentors themselves. [5]

If a boy does not have a mentor in his impressionable and formative years, when he craves male leadership and guidance the most, as a man he may be too proud to admit that he still has those needs. Often these unmet needs lead to feelings of anger, resentment, and insecurity. Without a healthy means of expression, these unmet needs do not have the opportunity to heal. As a result, they simply grow into bigger anger, bigger resentment, and bigger insecurity. Any wound left unattended can become infected and cause more damage. So many black men walk the streets, school hallways, and even high-rise office complexes suffering from unhealed and infected wounds that they try to treat with achievement, sex, drugs, and more money. Once we understand the internal pain, we understand why men sometimes are unwilling or unable to serve as mentors.

> *Over time boys get bigger, but without guidance, leadership, and mentoring, they often grow into bigger boys instead of strong men.*

When my son was three, I often asked him what he wanted to be when he grew up, and he always said, "Big." To him, being big meant you were grown up, but there is more to growing up than your size. Over time boys get bigger, but without guidance, leadership, and mentoring, they often grow into bigger boys instead of strong men. One of the most important truths we can instill in boys is that being a big man has very little to do with physical stature. Boys need a mentor to demonstrate that being big is more about characteristics such as standing up for what you believe in, being a man of your word, and serving others. As mentors, we need to show young men that what makes you a strong man is developing big, strong character more than big, strong muscles.

As we have already discussed, young men need mentors and models to help them navigate the ups and downs of life. However, to build strong black men, it is important to remember that the mentor-mentee relationship remains a critical part of growth and development throughout life. Mentoring should not stop when the boy turns eighteen. In fact, we cannot assume that just because a boy has turned eighteen he has been sufficiently mentored. In chapter 1, we discussed that many African cultures have rites of passage for the stages in a

---

5 David Miller, http://daretobeking.net/ (Retrieved December 14, 2012).

young man's life. Some cultures even have rites for older men, which take the young man through marriage and his own initiation into fatherhood. Once the boy becomes a man, he still needs other men in his life to offer continued support in his maturation process.

You don't need a mentor because you are weak; you need a mentor because no one is *that* strong alone. We were made to live in relationship and community with others. Even successful athletes who compete in individual sports, such as tennis, golf, or boxing, have a team of coaches, trainers, and supporters working with them. Great political leaders and CEO's of successful companies work with other talented people to help them achieve the glowing success we see. If the team approach works in politics, business, and sports, why should it be different in our lives? As a black man, I have often felt the need to make it on my own. My lack of having a father involved in my life produced a pride and a determination to show my father, and the world, that I could make it without him. Pride is one of the most common voices that men struggle with. Pride causes us to refuse to ask for directions even when we are lost. It prevents us from admitting that we are wrong when we are in an argument. It hinders us from being honest about our weaknesses, and it keeps us from disclosing that we need help.

As men, we need to seek mentors for ourselves so that we can be stronger for those we mentor. You can be a mentor even if you still have rough edges. The key is to have a mentor to help smooth them out along the way. It is a paradigm shift for a man who is not accustomed to male authority to consider receiving feedback and even guidance from another man. We may have to battle with pride, and maybe even some latent anger will arise and attempt to tell us that we have to make it without help. How do we mentor men who are well past the age of eighteen but just as needy for leadership and guidance? Let's discuss three key areas where men must receive the guidance and leadership provided by the mentoring process: faith and morality; professional life; and marriage and family.

## Faith and Moral Mentorship

Men need someone who will be honest and will wrestle with the tough spiritual questions, like "Is there a God?" "What if I struggle in my beliefs or have questions?" "Does anybody

*Remember, you don't have to force your beliefs when you live your beliefs.*

care about my morality beyond my routine religious behavior?" With the rise in what some call spiritual abuse perpetrated by pastors, priests, and other spiritual leaders, it's no wonder there is skepticism associated with men of faith. Why do men of faith cheat on their taxes and their significant other? Why do men of faith speak with such elegance in public, yet find themselves doing the most diabolical things in private? Why do men of faith leverage their position and power to use and abuse men, women, and children for their own gratification? The answer to these questions rests in the need men have for faith and moral mentorship.

Men *don't* need a demigod figure that tells them what to do and believe. They *do* need an honest man who has made mistakes, but has found a place of security in his own faith. Many black men who have been hurt by a lack of male leadership don't respond well to a man who tries to force beliefs on them. Remember, you don't have to force your beliefs when you live your beliefs.

Men are visual learners. Even though your mentee will hear what you say, he will focus more on what you actually *do*. Seeing is believing and men need to *see* real men modeling morality and faith in everyday life. Men need to see other men remaining faithful to their wives and families, even in the face of the temptation to do otherwise. Men need to see a man who knows what he believes, regardless of what others think or believe about him.

Accountability is important as we continue our journeys deeper into our development as men. Regardless of how strong and disciplined we are, we are human and often grow weary in the responsibilities and rigor of our daily routine. It is easy to lose sight of our values, and we often hear of a surprise divorce, a longtime struggle with an addiction, or business practices that are far less than aboveboard.

Find a spiritual mentor in your place of worship, your family, or a community organization. Even if you are not a man of a particular faith tradition, find someone who is willing to listen, is honest, and has your best interest in mind. Sometimes you may have to dig back into your past to reconnect with a former coach, teacher, or family friend, but by all means, begin this process.

## Professional Mentoring

*You work with your mentee; you don't do the work for your mentee.*

Once we are successful in helping our young men make it to and through college or into a particular vocation, we can't forget that they still need guidance. They need help as they grow in their chosen profession. After starting my private counseling practice, I felt lost because my degree program did not offer any courses in entrepreneurship or business development. My efforts to reach out for guidance from other black men in my profession were often met with vague generalities such as "Just work hard" and "Stay focused, and it will come together." What do those statements mean? I am not sure why they were not willing or able to answer specific questions, but I needed guidance and direction. In his book, *Success Runs in Our Race,* George C. Fraser wrote:

*Too many of us who have achieved success have turned our backs on urban America and those who remain mired in the cycle of underclass hopelessness. Too many of us have succumbed to the lazy philosophy that one person could not possibly make a difference in the lives of those who are still searching for a way out. ... Ultimately, it is up to those black people who have attained success to take on the moral responsibility to reach down and lift up their own. We are responsible for our own success or failure.*

As my network grew, my connection to other black men in my profession grew as well. Those professional relationships were invaluable to my development. Staying connected to professional mentors is vital as you offer mentorship to other professionals. I provide specific guidance when men ask me about becoming a counselor, obtaining a counseling license, or starting a practice. I am able to give them clear and candid feedback because of my mistakes and the many lessons I've learned. Mistakes can offer value if we learn from them. It is pointless to allow someone to make needless mistakes when you can offer them some of your personal knowledge and expertise as a resource. As a mentor, you provide guidance. You work with your mentee; you don't do the work for your mentee.

In his book *Mentoring 101*, renown leadership guru John Maxwell suggests mentors utilize the following process to develop strong mentees who will ultimately possess the fortitude to mentor others effectively:

- *I do it.* First I learn to do the job. I have to understand the why as well as the how, and I try to perfect my craft.
- *I do it—and you watch.* I demonstrate it while you observe, and during the process, I explain what I'm doing and why.
- *You do it—and I watch.* As soon as possible, we exchange roles. I give you permission and authority to take over the job, but I stay with you to offer advice, correction, and encouragement.
- *You do it.* Once you're proficient, I step back and let you work alone. The learner is drawn up to a higher level.[6]

It is always good to have a person who has more experience and has already blazed the trails you are currently treading. Sometimes it is not easy for us to invite the input of other men. It is especially difficult if you have not had a father or other male authority figure model this practice. However, professional and work mentorship is another key piece to helping black men develop and maintain thriving careers, businesses, and entrepreneurial ventures. To our readers who are currently in search of a professional mentor, we would like to offer some ideas for how to acquire a mentor for your professional and career development.

---

6 John Maxwell, Mentoring 101, Thomas Nelson, (2008).

- Attend national conferences and follow up with others you meet. Follow-up is key.
- Join associations related to your profession and attend local chapter meetings of your professional organizations to develop a local professional network (sign up for their newsletters and other communications).
- Participate in conference calls or webinars, because often you can ask questions of others in your area of interest. Form virtual networks with others on the call or webinar, if possible.
- When you hear a stunning and inspiring keynote speaker, instead of waiting in line to speak to him or her, use that time to introduce yourself to others who also attended the event. You never know who you might meet.
- Seek out continuing education opportunities in your field of work. You will always want to connect with others who are learning with you.
- Don't give up if you feel ignored or brushed off. Continue to seek a mentor.
- As you are seeking a mentor, be ready to offer your help and expertise to others who may be seeking your guidance. Be a mentor in areas that you know.

Finding a mentor may not happen overnight, and the most important key of all is to keep trying and follow up on every meeting, business card exchange, and handshake. We have already discussed the value in black men having mentorship in terms of their faith and the necessity for mentoring in their work and career development. Now let's focus specifically on the need for men to have mentors in the area of marriage and family.

## Marriage and Family Mentorship

Is marriage just for white people? This question has been debated and discussed in the *New York Times*, in *Time* magazine, in books, on talk shows, and elsewhere. Joy Jones, an educator, writer, and speaker, wrote a provocative article published in the *Washington Post* that depicted a conversation she had with her students about fatherhood and marriage. One young man affirmed his desire to be a strong father, but Jones highlighted the candid and ominous words of another twelve-year-old, who declared, "Marriage is for white people!" His words reveal the continued brokenness and fragmentation in the black family unit. [7] Solidarity in the black family is lacking, which is why this third key area of mentorship for black men is perhaps the most crucial of all. Black men who are married, or who aspire to marry, have a desperate need for mentorship in marriage and family. It is important to see living examples of how to build strong and lasting marriages and families.

---

7 Joy Jones, Is Marriage for White People? The Washington Post. http://www.washingtonpost.com/wp-dyn/content/article/2006/03/25/AR2006032500029.html (Retrieved January 8, 2013).

When I was growing up, my best friend's father served as an excellent example of a husband and father. I felt like a part of their family, and he was a great model for me since I did not have a father in my home. He served as a tangible example of the fact that black men *do* stay in the lives of their family members and they *do* provide love and leadership. Even now, he continues to serve as a model as he and his wife have celebrated over four decades of marital success. In fact, I saw very few examples, but his example gave me hope and an ideal to aspire to. Mentors in the area of marriage and family may be hard to find, but they do exist. You may have to sift through the stereotypes, but they are there. You may need to look deep into your extended family, but they are there. You may need to search deep into the annals of black history, but they are there. When you mentor a young man, you are not only mentoring that young man, but you are also facing the future of the black family.

## The Black Family: Hope Is Still an Option

Much of the motivation for this book has been a sober awakening to the reality that black men need to step up, grow up, and *man up*. However, we have to acknowledge that it will take an intentional effort to focus on facing our future and helping the next generation of black men be the strong leaders and providers that black women will aspire to marry. Our work has to focus on the future. If my daughters choose to marry black men, I hope that the energy and efforts inspired by this book will give them viable options. If my son one day becomes a husband and father it is my desire that he be the strong, black man that we are striving to produce. The legacy of the black family of tomorrow rests in the work we do to build strong black men today. If we want stronger black families, we need stronger black men. The way we develop stronger black men is to invest our time while they are boys and mentor them. Whatever qualities and virtues we want our boys to develop must be instilled and built into their lives. We are investing in the future because the impact we make in the lives of young black men will impact the sons and daughters that they one day bring into the world. We have to begin the work of turning the tide in a positive direction by investing in boys today so that they will reinvest in their children and families tomorrow.

> *The legacy of the black family of tomorrow rests in the work we do to build strong black men today.*

We have discussed the importance of identifying boys in our communities who need mentorship, and we have encouraged men to create mentoring programs. However, if you do not feel equipped to create your own program, below is a list of existing programs that you can plug into.

## Organizations With Mentoring Programs

### 100 Black Men Of America

*Mission:* to improve the quality of life within our communities and enhance educational and economic opportunities for all African Americans.
www.100blackmen.org
http://www.100blackmen.org/mentoring.aspx

### Big Brothers Big Sisters of America

*Mission:* to provide children facing adversity with strong and enduring, professionally supported, one-to-one relationships that change their lives for the better, forever.
www.bbbs.org

### Mentoring Brothers in Action

*Mission:* to engage more African American men in fraternal, social, faith-based, and professional organizations to get involved in one-to-one mentoring to change the odds for African American boys. This is a movement led by Big Brothers Big Sisters and the nation's three largest African American fraternities: Alpha Phi Alpha, Kappa Alpha Psi, and Omega Psi Phi.
www.mentoringbrothers.org

### Concerned Black Men

*Mission:* to provide guidance, support, and encouragement to children, while stabilizing families, positioning them to lead healthy, productive lives.
http://www.cbmnational.org/

### Dare To Be King Project

*Mission:* The mission of the Dare To Be King Project LLC (DTBK) is to inspire, support and strengthen organizations that provide services to boys of color. Our goal is to engage boys and men of color for emotional development, familial reconciliation and academic success.
Founded by David Miller, M.Ed., who developed the *MAN UP: Recruiting And Retaining African American Male Mentors* survey.
http://daretobeking.net/mentor-training/

## Mentoring National CARES Mentoring Movement

*Mission:* to recruit and retain one million mentors. After it was launched by Susan Taylor (former editor of *Essence* magazine) in 2007, a national initiative developed.

http://www.caresmentoring.org/

# Action Steps

*Are you willing to serve as a mentor for young black men?*

*What challenges will you have to overcome?*

*How can you overcome them?*

*When and where can you get started?*

# 3
# The Man Of The House

*Don't make a baby if you can't be a father.*
*-National Urban League Slogan*

We would like to begin this chapter by highlighting the fact that black men have owned their responsibilities to raise their children and lead their families for generations. As a culture, we have dedicated an enormous amount of time to the discussion of the issues related to fatherless homes while dropping the infamous statistics related to single parenting in the black community. Here we would rather focus on offering solutions.

When a man operates in his appropriate role as a leader and authority figure, the family prospers and dysfunction is reduced. Mothers are not forced to carry the childrearing responsibilities alone. Thank God for the presence of grandparents, aunts, uncles, godparents, foster parents, and mentors that fill in the gaps, but the impact of a biological father's presence is immeasurable, no matter how stable the child's home environment appears to be. Many of the issues related to the black family today could be solved if we could fix the fatherhood crisis. It is our opinion that if the statistics related to single parenthood were reversed, the media may not have much bad news to highlight in the black community. In this chapter, we will highlight the importance of the *visible* man, and what a father's presence versus his absence means to his children.

We've all heard the phrase "It takes two to tango." If it's obvious that it takes a man and a woman to conceive a child, it should be just as obvious that it will take a man and a woman to raise and nurture that child. Instead of discussing yesterday's news regarding the need for fathers to "show up," we'd like to spend the next couple of pages celebrating those that never left and discussing what absent fathers can do upon their return. Later we'll also discuss a child's

*When a man operates in his appropriate role as a leader and authority figure, the family prospers and dysfunction is reduced.*

need for both parents, explore the topic of effective co-parenting, and address the reality of teen fatherhood and how we can help these young men raise their children.

## The Visible Man—Growing Up in a Father-Led Home

During my elementary school years, I thought my dad, at six feet four inches, was the tallest man in the world. My father, who is now enjoying retirement, was a very accomplished soldier who honorably served our country as a first sergeant in the National Guard. We would often visit the commissary in Fort Bragg, North Carolina, during my childhood. On one particular visit, my family was standing in the general shopping area when a group of soldiers in uniform walked by. Now, I had seen tons of soldiers before, but one of the men stood out immediately because of his tree-like stature. Standing there in complete shock, repeatedly comparing the top of his head to my father's, I estimated he was a full five inches taller. This was a moment of truth for me. Literally. Like most young men at that age, my thoughts and beliefs were shaped by my exposure. I realized in that moment that my dad was no longer the tallest man in the world. He was the tallest man in *my* world!

It was impossible for me to deny what I saw with my own eyes, but at that age, the immeasurable daily impact of my dad's presence, love, provision, and guidance far outweighed the mere five inches of height that were out of his control. He was no longer the tallest man in the world. But he was still the tallest example of a real man I'd ever come in contact with. This made all the difference.

As a young black man, I didn't always realize just how fortunate I was to live in a two-parent, father-led household. The stability that stems from two adults that genuinely love one another and are fully committed to building a family together is more beneficial than these pages allow me to detail. When I was a child, it was very easy for me to assume that everyone else came from a two-parent household just like mine. However, nothing could be further from the truth.

I remember when one of my schoolmates, another black male, accused me of being rich. Even at a young age, I had a perception of what I believed rich was. He used examples such as my clothing to support his point. This was a little confusing to me, because unless my parents were keeping a huge secret from my sister and I, we weren't exactly rich according to the material definition he was applying. My sister and I were very fortunate to have parents that were excellent providers. They taught us to represent ourselves, and the family, well in public. As I reflect back on some of those tense moments as an adolescent, I tend to agree with my former classmate. I *was* rich! I was rich in love, support, security, and positive self-esteem. When I was born, my father and mother had already been married ten years. I was privileged to benefit from the commitment of two adults who were vested in their marriage: having pledged their lives to one another, and were committed to building a strong legacy of family that had been passed down to them by their parents.

The legacy we're speaking of is that of a father being present and committed to working with the mother to keep the family unit together. We understand that some marriages or relationships are unsalvageable. However, regardless of the differences between father and mother, both individuals will be parents forever. Your status as a parent is not optional; however, the quality of your parenting is within your complete control. You can be an awful parent or a great parent; an absent parent or a present parent. The choice is yours.

Many young black men are fortunate to have what others are often forced to grow up without, due to no fault of their own. You've probably heard the saying "There are no illegitimate children, just illegitimate parents." In other words, many children are born to biological parents who had no intentions of becoming parents when they decided to *tango*. The child is not at fault, but when parents forsake their individual and collective responsibilities to work together to raise their child, it's usually the child that

> *Your status as a parent is not optional; however, the quality of your parenting is within your complete control.*

suffers most. Over the next few pages, let's continue to discuss the immeasurable benefits of intentional fatherhood as it relates to building strong black men.

## The Benefits and Values of Fatherhood

*Identity.* A lot of a young man's struggle stems from the lack of affirmation that normally would come from a father or father figure. There is nothing quite like the blessing of a father. Young men need some messages about identity to come specifically from their father. In the family structure, the father is the leader, provider, protector, and counselor. It is a father's responsibility to tell a young man who he is and to empower him with the mental, emotional, physical, and spiritual support that he needs to understand his value and purpose in life. However, to do this, first the father has to know who he is. If the father grew up without his father, the lack of stability and confusion could very well continue on to the next generation. The reality is, 67 percent of black children are being born into single-parent homes. There are certainly fathers who are the primary caregivers for their children, but in many cases, child rearing falls into the lap of the mother. [8]

---

8 National KIDS COUNT. CHILDREN IN SINGLE-PARENT FAMILIES BY RACE. Kids count Data center. http://datacenter.kidscount.org/data/tables/107-children-in-single-parent-families-by#detailed/1/any/false/868,867,133,38,35/10,168,9,12,1,13,185,11/432,431 (Retrieved on March 15, 2013).

*Validation.* Growing up in a father-led home allowed me to experience a healthy measure of emotional stability. My father's constant presence left no room for deliberation as to whether my mother, sister, and I were "good enough" or "worthy" of his attention. Black children need their fathers to affirm and validate them in the home early and often. My father and mother took great care to make sure that my sister and I were aware of our value as people. They affirmed us inside the home with lessons of humility and self-confidence, such as "Never think you are better than anyone else, but always know that you're just as good as anyone else."

> *It is a father's responsibility to tell a young man who he is and to empower him with the mental, emotional, physical, and spiritual support that he needs to understand his value and purpose in life.*

*Protection and security.* Being the "man of the house" is the responsibility of the father. There are obviously situations where young black men may be counted on to step up because the father works irregular hours or travels extensively because of his vocation. There are also males who were born into father-led homes, but the father is deceased. These particular scenarios may create a necessity for a young man to take on the role of protector for his family. However, when a young black man is able to observe his father, or a father-figure, operate in the role of man of the house, he is better equipped to understand how to provide the same protection and security for his own family. To become strong black men, young men must be nurtured in environments where they feel safe and secure.

*Father-and-son bonding projects.* Growing up in a father-led home provides a tremendous advantage for the young black male who will likely grow up to lead a household of his own. I can speak from personal experience and say that I learned a lot of things through father-and-son talks, various home improvement projects, and the frequent, and often informal, interactions that happen between a man and his son over the course of childhood and adolescence. Many things are *caught*, not taught. By observing my father, I internalized a strong sense of responsibility, as well as the value and pride in hard work. Below is a partial list of things I feel fortunate to have learned from my dad prior to adulthood by tagging along (even when I didn't feel like it), asking questions, and curiously peeping over his shoulder. Through these experiences, many of which were "on-the-job training," I learned how to:

- Ride a bike
- Landscape
- Drive a car
- Change a flat tire
- Check an automobile's fluid levels

- Lay brick
- Build a storage facility
- Install appliances
- Shave
- Install a basketball goal
- Treat a woman respectfully

You might be saying to yourself, "A child could actually learn to do a lot of those things by watching a man, a woman, or even YouTube videos." However, as an adult, it is priceless to be able to reflect on these lessons learned in my youth at the hands of my father. These experiences produced vivid memories and critical one-on-one time for my father to communicate to me man-to-man.

Looking back, I realize that these projects were about so much more than the task at hand. Learning how to ride a bike was also a lesson in facing my fears head-on and trusting my instincts. Falling off a bike produced the opportunity to learn from my dad about how to bounce back from a failure. I was always taught that the driver of a vehicle is not only responsible for his life, but also for the lives of the passengers in the vehicle with him. Learning to drive and earning the privilege to operate the family cars was a test of my level of responsibility as much as it was about developing good driving technique. Building a storage facility was about learning how to work with a partner or as a part of a team. It taught me how to manage a project from start to finish, to be attentive to details, and to challenge myself to try new things. Through these projects, I developed good work habits and self-confidence, and I learned how to make myself more marketable through the acquisition of new skills and talents.

*Establishing values and proper priorities.* If you were to ask most principals or teachers which parent is most likely to express concern about the academic welfare of a student, most would say the mother. We are not attempting to diminish the importance of the mother's presence, but as a child, seeing your father show up at different events is a big deal. When I was growing up, my father never worked in the same city that we lived in. When he arrived at my school for a parent-teacher conference, an athletic event, or an awards ceremony, it was usually after making a forty-five minute drive from work. This communicated that what was important to me was also important to him and to the entire family. It was often discouraging to see the fathers of many of my young black male students religiously attend basketball and football games, and just a few nights later, be missing in action on parent-teacher conference night to discuss the same child's academic performance. This can give a message that athletics are important to men and academics are important to women. Nothing could be further from the truth! If we want to build strong black men, we must help them to establish values and priorities around things that will have a direct impact on their trajectory in life, such as their education.

*Discipline.* My father was the lead disciplinarian in the home when I was a child. My mother was tough on my sister and me as well. We certainly didn't want anyone, such as a teacher or school administrator, to say the words, "I'm going to call your parents." I would have rather waxed their car with a toothbrush! But, in the case of far too many young black males today, the words "I'm going to call your mama!" mean absolutely nothing. Please don't misunderstand. We are very thankful for all the women who are fulfilling their commitment to raise their sons in the absence of their fathers. However, there are some good women who, though they mean well, love their sons to dysfunction—and in some cases, to death. This may be because they are physically afraid of their sons. Even if they are not afraid of him, they may be afraid of his poor decision-making skills. They also may feel helpless because they were not raised to be a man, but a woman, so their perspective about manhood is based on opinion, not experience.

> *Fathers must be present to show love, to teach, and apply discipline to their sons to help them reach their full potential as black men.*

The black community must address the leniency of some mothers toward their sons. In his book entitled *Understanding Black Male Learning Styles*, Dr. Jawanza Kunjufu refers to this as "mothers raising their daughters and loving their sons." [9] In other words, black girls learn to be responsible and self-sufficient by watching and learning from their mothers. These girls often grow up to be powerful, educated, and upwardly mobile black women capable of taking care of themselves. In the same household, their brothers, who should be learning to be strong black men from their father or a positive male mentor, are often sheltered and protected by their mothers. The father's absence creates an unhealthy attachment between mother and son, which can ultimately cause the young black male to be spoiled, lazy, unproductive, and dependent upon women for his survival. As an educator, I've witnessed many single and married mothers of young black men attempt to "cover" for their adolescent son's irresponsible behavior. This often occurred in the form of them making excuses for the young man's inappropriate conduct and blaming teachers for their sons' grades instead of holding the young man accountable to higher academic standards. The adult version of this young black man still aspires to live at home with his mother at thirty and is severely unfit to be the husband to any of the single black women who were actually *raised* by their mothers. This should never be considered acceptable in black society! Fathers must be present to show love, to teach, and apply discipline to their sons to help them reach their full potential as black men.

---

9 Jawanze Kunjufu, Understanding Black Male Learning Styles (African American Images, 2010).

*The importance of family.* Being raised in a father-led home allowed me to gain a greater understanding of the importance of family. Family time such as nightly dinners, vacations, birthdays, and holiday celebrations created the opportunity to feel the joy and power of the family unit as led by the father. Participating in discussions with both my father and mother allowed my sister and me to hear and process issues from both the male and the female perspective. During those times, we learned how to communicate successfully with adults and our peers. Thus I learned values and was able to form and voice socially conscious opinions about many different topics, including education, religion, world events, politics, relationships, sports, and many other things families should discuss so that young black men can become well-rounded human beings.

## Apples Don't Fall Far from the Tree

Another tremendous advantage of the father-led home is that you get to know both the paternal and maternal sides of your extended family. You are able to trace your history and discover more about yourself. All fruit falls from trees with many different branches and deeply planted roots. There is no better testament to the legacy of the father-led home than the fruit produced via healthy, stable relationships with grandparents, uncles, aunts, and cousins. I was privileged to meet and to share considerable time with my paternal and maternal grandparents. I was named after my father, who also came from a two-parent, father-led home. My maternal grandfather's name was Garfield Casteen Joyce. He was a devoted husband and father to six beautiful girls. He was a hard worker, never met a stranger, always wore a gigantic smile, and was a leader in the community. He was such a staple in the local community that the city named the street that he resided on "Garfield Street." Honored as a legend while he was alive, he is still the only person I've ever met who actually lived on the street that was named in his honor. Giving was a way of life for him, and charity always began at home.

The further we go back into black history, the more likely we are to find two-parent homes. Here's an interesting black history fact: in the early 1920s, it was rare to find a black family that was not a two-parent home.[10] My paternal grandfather, the Reverend Zack R. Reynolds, was born in 1916, and his father died when he was only seven years old. He had a unique experience in that he grew up without his father in a time when most families were led by both parents. As the only male child in a household full of women (he had six sisters), he assumed the role and mental disposition of "man of the house." Even as he grew into an adult without his biological father's presence, he still internalized the value of the male taking an active role in the family structure. My paternal grandparents had ten children—five boys and five girls. My father was the oldest male child. He had

10 Steven Ruggles, The Origins of African-American Family Structure, American Sociological Review, 1994, Vol 59 (February: 136-151).

the privilege of learning how to work to provide for a family and the importance of having a good name and reputation in your local community by observing my grandfather, who made his living as a farmer.

We are better able to understand ourselves when we are aware of our history. In the process of writing this book, my father shared some things with me about his dad's mentality and approach to fatherhood. Ironically, both of my grandfathers passed away when I was nineteen years old. Their legacy continues to live on through my extended family members and me. Below are a few of the lessons learned from these strong black men.

## Lessons From My Grandfathers

- *Be your own man*. Men should think for themselves. Remember that blending in with a crowd is the quickest way to get lost in it.
- *Be self-sufficient*. My paternal grandfather equipped his children with the desire to support themselves and their families. An avid farmer who bought 111 acres of land in North Carolina during the South's peak era of racial unrest, he opted to raise his own crops to provide for his wife and ten children.
- *Be a hard worker.* Not only should men and fathers work, but they should also purpose to work diligently. If something is not worth working for, it's probably not worth having. There are some tasks that can be completed in minutes, but there are also tasks and visions that take days, weeks, months, and even years to complete. The key is to work with fervor and efficiency.
- *Face your fears and reality*. Life is not always pleasant, and there are challenges along the way. In order to overcome your fears, you must first be willing to confront them. You must be willing to take ownership of the results that come from your decisions. One of my grandfather's most memorable quotes about responsibility was "If you make your bed hard, you've still got to sleep in it."
- *Be a giver*. My grandfather planted more than enough. He always had enough to give away to someone else. This is a principle that both of my grandfathers lived by. And it doesn't play favorites; giving positions you to receive.
- *Be willing to take on a new challenge*. Fathers are leaders, and they are faced with challenges every day. Instead of shrinking away from new challenges and ventures, move forward. At the very least, you will learn something new. Only then will you know what you're capable of.

## I Don't Have a Daddy

When I was in elementary school, riding on the school bus, I told one of my peers that I did not have a daddy. The boy laughed and said, "Everybody has a daddy." He was right; everyone has a daddy because it is a biological necessity—but not every daddy is involved with his children. At that time, I remembered very little of my father, and because he did not live with us, I had internalized the idea that I did not have a father. After the incident on the school bus, I began to pay closer attention to the fact that living without a father in the home was not unique to me. Movies, sitcoms, daytime talk shows, and news reports verify the reality of the absent black father. The pervasiveness of homes without fathers in the black community gave birth to many negative stereotypes about black fathers and black boys raised without their dads in the home. The stereotypes told me that I should be a dropout and drug user or dealer; I should have multiple children by different mothers; I should spend time locked up; and I should live with my mother well into my thirties. But those negative images and stereotypes became a guide for me in that they informed me of what I did *not* want to become. I decided not to allow my absent father to become an excuse for me to end up a statistic. Much of my resolve was not self-made but came from seeing my mother's determination to support our family. She worked hard and provided for our needs, and I don't remember hearing her complain. My mother also used our extended family as a strong support network in our lives. My aunts, uncles, and grandmother reinforced the values of hard work and the importance of family.

I didn't know my father, but I did not feel a sense of loss, because my mother and extended family did an excellent job filling the void. They did such a great job that I felt like I'd beaten the statistics and the stereotypes. I remember church members, teachers, and other adults telling my mother that I was a fine young man. They commended her for the job she had done, and I felt proud. As a child, I never felt a sense of loss.

For all practical purposes, I did make it. I completed college, did not dabble in drugs and alcohol, did not participate in criminal behavior, and fathered no children outside of marriage. Not until I became a father did I feel the immeasurable loss of not knowing my own father. I learned to be a man from coaches, male family members, and other positive teachers, counselors, and mentors. But *nothing* prepared me for fatherhood. I had not had the model of a man in the home. I did not know my father's passion, his pain, his successes, or his failures.

I began to feel that loss when I was asked to complete a simple checklist at one of my daughter's first doctor's appointments. It had questions about my family medical history. With ease I recounted the history of my mother and maternal grandparents, but I could not contribute any information about my father or my paternal grandparents. Because I never knew my father, I had only half of the story. I could not help my daughter's doctor understand my father's medical history, which had a direct impact on my children and me.

I know nothing of my paternal side of the family, and I now feel the loss. I have never met my grandparents, aunts, or uncles. I cannot tell my children stories about their grandfather. I cannot reference the annals of my father's history to get advice for various problems or difficult decisions. I "made it" without my father, but as a man and a father myself, I recognize that my father's absence cost me a sense of who I am and what I will pass along.

I remember the first time my daughter asked about "Grandma's husband." I had to tell her that I did not know him. Once she figured out that Grandma's husband was my father, she seemed shocked and confused that I did not know him. "What do you mean, you don't know him?" I had to explain that I had not seen my father since I was very young and did not remember much about him.

Even if you don't know your father, here are some ideas for building and creating a sense of pride and identity in your children:

- Establish annual events such as cookouts or travel at certain times of the year.
- Create shared experiences such as road trips and campouts, even if your campsite is nothing more than the backyard. Memories are valuable and can be passed down.
- Take pictures of events, activities, and milestones; pictures always go well with good stories.
- Build pride and respect around your name, and establish a reputation that you want your children to uphold. Our young men need to know that a strong name is valuable and can carry them throughout their lives.
- Teach your children the values that you want them to carry on, such as working hard, taking responsibility for their actions, and respecting themselves and others.

## The Invisible Father

Being a new father was a difficult process for me; it was full of rude awakenings. The portrait of the black father that was presented to me as a boy was full of imperfections and defects. The image I most remember was that black men were sexually promiscuous and had children by different mothers but had little connection with *any* of their children. I often overheard my aunts and many of my mother's friends talking about how they wished black men would stand up and be strong fathers and leaders in the family.

It did not take me long to get the point. The perception was that we black men are not great fathers, and I had no father to show me otherwise. I struggled with this message and told myself that I would never have children, so that I did not have to confront potential failure as a father. On the other hand, if I did have children, I promised myself that I would be the opposite of the negative images of the black father that had been presented to me. Most of the time I pretended that I did not want children, but I secretly longed to grow into a man who would be a strong father and lead and love a strong family.

> *The absence of the black father is magnified, but his presence is often minimized, if not ignored altogether.*

I had no father as a model, so I did not know the role that a father *should* play in the lives of his children. All I knew was that I wanted to play an active role in my children's lives. Therefore, I was literally present at most everything involving my daughter, from doctor's appointments to day-care center visits to daddy-daughter dates. I was there! Since I was there, I began to notice that I was often invisible. When my wife and I were together, any questions or conversations about our daughter were *always* directed at her. It was rare if the person even looked at me. I will never forget one of our first doctor's appointments. Before we saw the doctor, the financial manager entered the room to shore up the particulars of our insurance. She immediately greeted my wife and started to discuss the insurance without even glancing my way. She acknowledged me only after I extended my hand to introduce myself. She looked surprised—almost distraught—that I would interrupt her routine and customary practice. I dismissed the doctor's visit as an anomaly and reasoned that the financial manager was just in a hurry and probably did not even see me. However, experiences like it became a shocking and disturbing norm in my experience as a new father. I found that my presence was almost an *annoyance*. I began to feel like people were thinking, *Why is he always around, and not only that, but why does he have to be so involved?* As a father, you have every right to be present. If you are ignored, simply introduce yourself and involve yourself in the conversation about your child.

When I was child, I was confused as I recalled the times that I'd heard about how black men ran out on their children and how absent fathers were destroying black families. Sometimes I heard the prevailing voice of society beg black men to step up and be fathers. Often this voice took the form of a daytime talk show that admonished fathers for not paying child support or for abandoning their children. At other times, this voice took the form of academicians who study the perils created by the absent black father. Regardless of its form, this voice was loud and clear: "Black men need to step up and be fathers to their children." I agreed with my whole heart that black men needed to step up, so I decided to step up. However, when my presence was consistently ignored, I was left thinking that the absence of the black father is magnified, but his presence is often minimized, if not ignored altogether. The talk shows, tabloids, and sensational media *need* black men to remain absent as fathers. Present and involved black fathers are not exciting or sensational. They stop the "baby daddy" drama in its tracks. Frankly, present and involved black fathers are bad for ratings and bad for business.

Black men are admonished when they run out and are absent, but what do those same admonishing voices do with the black father who is present in his child's life? My experience led me to believe that those same voices sought to arrest my parental involvement and read me my rights: "You have the right to remain absent. In fact, we need you to remain absent, so we can sensationalize it and further demoralize black men in America." If you are a father and feel invisible, here are some tips:

- *Focus on your family*. Your children will feel your impact and value your presence. It really does not matter how others view you.
- *Politely assert your presence*. If you are ignored, simply introduce yourself; speak up and remind others that you are there.
- *Seek to connect with other fathers who share your family commitment*. It is always good to have encouragement and to be reminded that you are not alone. You can build each other up, especially when circumstances are trying to tear you down.

## Happy Tie Day!

Mothers are a true blessing and deserve honor and esteem. My wife's first Mother's Day was a glorious celebration. Cards and calls showered her throughout the day. Judging from the clamor, I think even our infant daughter knew that it was a very important day. I was accustomed to celebrating Mother's Day, and I was doubly blessed to celebrate with both my wife and my mother.

You can imagine my excitement to celebrate my first Father's Day. I thought that a present black father was something to celebrate. I celebrated with my wife and daughter, which are the only two who really mattered, but I was expecting more. I waited all day, no cards, no calls, and only one voicemail that came so late in the evening I did not even check it until after the fact.

As I consulted with other fathers, they laughed and explained that Father's Day is typically not that big of a deal. They even joked about how they bought their father a tie every year as more of a routine than an expression of love and appreciation. Then it hit me; most of my friends grew up with fathers in the home. Perhaps it was only significant to me because I never had the experience of celebrating, and I was not aware of the apparent lack of emphasis on Father's Day.

As a person who grew up hearing and seeing so much negativity surrounding black fathers, I held out a hope that it would change for the better. I decided to stop feeling sorry for myself and to do something to change the image of fatherhood in my family. I wanted to give my children a vision of fatherhood that extended beyond the perfunctory gifts, and I wanted them to see that fatherhood is a reason to celebrate. I organized and established a tradition I called the annual FDC (Father's Day Cookout). It is a time to gather family and friends to celebrate. We celebrate fathers and the institution of fatherhood. We intentionally highlight the importance of fathers. The FDC is a simple cookout, but it is now an annual tradition in our family that my children will at least have as a model if they choose to carry it on one day.

## Provide, Protect, and Parent

My wife is a registered nurse, and when our children were very young, she often worked weekend shifts. I was off on the weekends, so I naturally cared for our children. When anyone came to visit or called our house and found out that my wife was not home, the first words out

> *Parenting includes being involved with the discipline, education, and the health of our children.*

of their mouths were "So I see you are babysitting today?" When I first started hearing that question, I did not know how to answer. *Babysitting? How can I babysit my own children? Are you serious?* Now I simply say, "No, I am not babysitting, I am parenting!"

Society has accepted the mandate that fathers in general are supposed to provide for the family. The provision that is expected is of a financial nature. The next traditional expectation is that we are responsible to protect. We are supposed to use our strength to keep our families safe from physical dangers. However, in the twenty-first century, gender roles are changing. There was a time when men did not even go to the hospital when their children were born. Now fathers help support the mother during the childbirth process, cut the cord, and are a part of the entire experience. Parenting includes being involved with the discipline, education, and the health of our children. As mothers work, as my wife did on the weekends, fathers are responsible for much of the child-rearing responsibilities.

As black fathers, it is important that we remain present in our children's lives. If you are a black man and you have children, your input in the everyday affairs is important. Fathers are parents, and it is just as important for us to read to our children, be aware of our children's health, and know our children's age and birthdates. Our children need us. Here are some important things we need to do as parents to meet our children's needs:

- *Be emotionally engaged.* They need us to emerge from our emotional man cave and to be emotionally awake. It is easy and often expected that men will express anger, but our children need us to express other emotions, such as fear and sadness. Otherwise, young men grow up thinking they are weak or not a real man when they experience these normal human emotions. Often they experience our anger, but they need to see our compassion and our ability to express ourselves without aggression.
- *Listen.* We talk to our children and provide direction and guidance, but there are times when our children need us to simply listen to their needs

and concerns. They don't always need us to solve problems and fix their messes. Listening is a gift that gives our children a voice.

- *Spend quality time with them.* Children can tell when you are really engaged with them and when you really just want to watch the game. Set aside time when your children can have your undivided attention.
- *Speak words of encouragement and life.* My daughter learned a song for her school play when she was in kindergarten, and the chorus went something like this: "Words can hurt; be careful what you say. Think before you speak; there is a better way." Words have power and meaning, so it is important that our words to our children build them up, because they are living in a world that can easily tear them down.
- *Support their dreams.* They need us at their sporting events, their music recitals, and their various graduations. Years ago I attended a men's event, and the main speaker talked about the profound impact it had on him when he found out that his father was at every one of his football games. His father had kept up with his stats, but his son never knew until he reconciled with his father as an adult. His father was able to recall specific details about specific games that he could have known only by attending the games. The speaker exclaimed that he would have made it to the National Football League if he had known his father was there all along.
- *Become an expert in the things that are important to them*. If it is art, music, math, or science, learn more about the areas that are important to them. You will be able to talk with them about those topics or even participate in some of the activities. This helps build connection.

## Cooperative Co-Parenting vs. Parallel Parenting

> *Divorce severs the marriage relationship, but you cannot divorce your children; they will always be your children.*

In an ideal world, the father and mother would live together as husband and wife and raise their children together. However with the divorce rate at 50 percent, the ideal two-parent home is not a reality for everyone. Please note that just because a child lives in a one-parent home does not mean he or she has to live without two parents. Divorce severs the marriage relationship, but you cannot divorce your children; they will always be your children. Not living with your child does not mean you cannot parent and invest in your child's life. It will take effort, and it may not be easy, but your child is worth the energy. If you are a father who wants to be involved in your child's life, try to work toward cooperative parenting as opposed to parallel parenting, which is a common practice. Cooperative co-parenting works in the best interest of the child. The distinctions between the two styles are shown in the chart below.

| Cooperative Co-Parenting | Parallel Parenting |
|---|---|
| Parents communicate freely and directly | Parents communicate little. They do communicate directly in emergencies |
| Parenting plans more general and flexible | Parenting plans must be specific and more rigid |
| Direct transfers of children | Neutral transfers of children |
| The two households work cooperatively | The two households are totally independent |
| Differing parenting styles are discussed | No discussion of parenting styles |
| Meetings may be informal | Meetings must be formal and scheduled |
| More focused on the child | More focused on the parents |
| No need for a third party | Third party authorities are needed to work out concerns |

Again, though many black fathers do not live with their child that does not mean they are excused from being involved in the lives of their children. Cooperative co-parenting takes work but it benefits the child in the long run.

## Babies Making Babies

During my high school years, I heard the phrase "babies having babies." It was mostly used in youth rallies at my church to describe girls who had gotten pregnant in their early teens. The speaker had good intentions, because he was encouraging us to stay focused on school and our spiritual lives, but his attention seemed to always be diverted to the topic of teenage pregnancy. Perhaps the rather large group of teenage mothers in our church prompted the "impromptu" admonitions, but he almost never made it back to his speech about spirituality.

As I reflect on it, the youth of our church may have been better served if the leaders had just told us up front about the importance of abstinence and safe and responsible sexual practice. I remember that much of the emphasis was placed on the young women, because they were the ones carrying the children. I always thought, *I wonder who the fathers are?* They could have been young men in the room, but if they were in the room, they were never identified. I also remember thinking that the topic of babies having babies was of great significance because, in addition to hearing about it from leaders of our youth ministry, I saw news reports, read newspaper articles, and listened to talk shows dealing with the same topic. Of course, those young women didn't get pregnant alone. Not only were babies (young women) having babies, but babies (young men) were also helping to make babies. The commentary about babies having babies was not much more than rhetoric to me until I started counseling young men. I have worked with many teenage fathers, but one in particular stands out to me. He was only thirteen when he conceived his son, but he talked about being responsible and taking care of his child. However, he had very few resources that would allow him to do that. To his credit, he wanted to provide and he wanted to be involved in his son's life. As a result, I was able to help him problem solve and develop some obtainable goals to help him stay connected to his son.

Unfortunately, many of the teenage fathers I have counseled still have the mindset of a teen and are not aware of the grave nature of their new parental responsibilities. The sense of urgency became stronger for me during a treatment team meeting with a young man I served in the juvenile justice system. (To provide a comprehensive and thorough system of care, the program I worked with conducted monthly treatment team meetings.) The young man's aunt, social worker, a psychologist, and a probation officer were in attendance. Each of them tried in earnest to discourage his practice of unprotected sex. Despite their most compelling arguments and urgings, he insisted that one of the first things he was going to do when he left the facility was get someone pregnant. His rationale was that he wanted to have a cute baby that looked like him. He appeared to have no sense of the dire nature of his statement as he casually talked about the baby's eye color, hair type, and complexion. When his team members asked how he would take care of a baby, he said casually that the mother of the child and her people would handle it.

How do we effectively address the problem? It is easy to reason that the solution is to teach abstinence or emphasize contraceptive use. Of course these are the most effective ways to avoid pregnancy. However, as noted earlier, the teen pregnancy rate continues to rise. Therefore, our message must reach the young men who have *not* abstained or used contraceptives and have become fathers.

## Mentoring for Teen Fathers

When I worked with young men at a Youth Development Center, I facilitated a parenting group with another therapist. We educated the young men about key elements of parenting, such as communication with the mother, dealing with stress and anger, and understanding the developmental stages of their babies from birth to preschool. We also included a component that addressed their personal concerns as teenage fathers. Here are key principles for such groups:

- *Include material on the basics of parenting.* These include reading to, disciplining, nurturing, and supporting the child. We want to make sure the young men understand the developmental milestones that their child would be experiencing. We also debunk the myth that fathers can't do much for their children until they are old enough to throw a football or shoot a basketball. We drive home the point that fatherhood begins at conception and does not end.
- *Have the young men address his child's mother as "the mother of my child."* Many young men have a difficult relationship with their child's mother. However, the tone and attitude of the young men changes once they refrain from referring to her as "my baby mama" and start referring to her as "the mother of my child." It gives the mother some dignity in their eyes and elevates her to the same place as their own mothers, whom many of them respect.
- *Explain that they can still be in their child's life even if they do not live in the same home.* Many teen fathers do not live permanently with their child due to the fact that they are not financially solvent enough to have their own home. Because of this, sometimes adolescent fathers feel they cannot be involved with their child. They may also feel pushed out of the child's life by the mother's family, who would prefer that he stay as far away as possible. It is difficult, but important to help young fathers learn to navigate these difficult relationships for the sake of having a relationship with their children.
- *Include an emphasis on self-development, which will ultimately benefit their child.* Just as adults are advised by airline personnel to put on their oxygen masks first and then assist small children, it is important that an adolescent father continues to grow personally. We need to assist him in furthering his education or acquiring additional skills in order to be more employable. If he is more employable or if he develops his own business, he will have more to offer his child.

Solutions for addressing the problems of teen fatherhood are still fairly new, but there are numerous programs that offer promise for our teen fathers. The body of research on what makes programs and resources for teen fathers successful is growing. Researchers with the National Responsible Fatherhood Clearinghouse published a study with a select number of teen fatherhood programs nationwide and identified the following as key components that made the programs more promising:

- Partnered with community organizations such as schools, prenatal clinics, and programs for teen mothers to help recruit and engage teen fathers
- Had program staff develop one-on-one relationships with teen fathers, either in small groups, through individual case management, or through mentoring services
- Offered a comprehensive array of services to teen fathers that went beyond parenting information
- Began with a theoretical program model and used theories of change or logic models that were effective with adolescent parents
- Delivered services in engaging and interactive ways
- Conducted needs assessments and/or used participant feedback to provide teen fathers the services they wanted
- Hired professionals who were experienced, empathetic, enthusiastic, well connected in the community, and carefully matched to participants
- Incorporated teaching methods and materials that were appropriate for teen fathers and their culture and age
- Used an incentive with teen fathers and their families
- Mentored teen fathers [11]

Adolescent fathers are in great need of support, and you can be a part of the solution. Please consider starting a program through your faith-based community or other community-based entities.

We had the opportunity to interview numerous young men while writing this book. One in particular stands out as an excellent example of being a young father and facing responsibilities with the courage and fortitude of a *real* man and a *real* father. Chris Matthews answered a variety of questions and offered advice and guidance for young fathers. He is currently married to the mother of his son and is a successful entrepreneur.

*What was your initial reaction when you discovered you were going to become a father?*
When my girlfriend told me she was pregnant, I was twenty years old and I was a college student. I told her that I would call her back. My brother told me to ask if it was my baby. I asked her if she was sure that it was my baby, and I felt her heart break. She answered with disgust in her voice and said yes. We considered getting an abortion but could not go through with it and decided to have the baby.

*Did you ever have doubts that you could be a great father? Why or why not?*
Yes, the doubts came after my son was born. The first time I had my son without my girlfriend, I was nervous and scared, and I did not know what to do. It was the first time I had to take into account someone else's needs on a 24/7 basis.

11 Jacinta Bronte-Tinkew, Ph.D., Mary Burkhauser, M.A., & Allison Metz, Ph.D., PROMISING TEEN FATHERHOOD PROGRAMS: INITIAL EVIDENCE LESSONS FROM EVIDENCE-BASED RESEARCH (2008).

*How did you handle the doubts?*
I focused on my relationship with my girlfriend. We developed a team focus. We supported each other.

*What has been your greatest challenge as a young father?*
My greatest challenge has been wearing the worries of my son. They are on me. I wear my heart on my sleeve. I question things like, "Is he at the right school?" "Is his development up to par?", "Am I reading to him every night?" and "How am I going to be viewed as a parent?"

*What do you tell a teen that finds out he is going to be a father?*
Learn to develop a relationship with the mother of your child. That relationship is valuable in the eyes of the court system. It is important to make sure you have access to your child. Often, it is not that black men want to walk away from their child, but they lose the connection because the mother often does not allow access. Access gets tough, and the man gives up.[12]

Here is some advice that can help young fathers:

**Share in the nurturing of your children**. It is important for black men to take an active role in the area of childcare. Share as much responsibility as you can with the child's mother, especially if you are the main breadwinner for the family and the mother is a stay-at-home mom or tends to take on most of the responsibility in this area.

> *The typical stereotypes of black men can dissolve if we stop supporting them with our absence.*

**Attend important events featuring your children**. Fathers should be present at all events featuring their children (childbirth, first day of school, recitals, parent-teachers nights, recognition ceremonies, church plays, etc.). This communicates to the child that all of his or her activities are important to you, not just athletic events. The typical stereotypes of black men can dissolve if we stop supporting them with our absence.

**Communicate with your children on a regular basis**. We live in an age when communication options are endless. There is absolutely no excuse for a father not to communicate with his children. We also strongly encourage face-to-face interaction, as opposed to communicating solely through phone calls, texting, and social media. You need to be able to look into your children's eyes when communicating with them, and they need to be able to look directly into yours. The eyes are the windows to the soul, and unless we are face-to-face, we miss out on all the meaning that is communicated through the eyes and body language.

---

12 Chris Matthews, interviewed by Jeremiah Hopes, Behavioral Health Intervention Center, February 6, 2013.

*Speak peaceably with the mother of your child.* You may not be married or in an intimate relationship anymore, but you will always be parents. Work hard at getting along with each other. You and the mother of your child are the only biological parents your children will ever have. Strive to make their thoughts about their parents' interpersonal interactions as positive as possible.

*Lean forward: Be the dad that's "present," not just "around."* As an accomplished soldier and veteran of the National Guard, my father told me that he encouraged his soldier trainees to "lean forward" in their foxhole. In other words, to properly engage the enemy while in combat, a soldier must lean forward and seek out targets. Like soldiers in combat, black men can't afford to be passive and timid in the territory of fatherhood. A strong black man must lean forward to engage and defeat the enemies of apathy toward his children, poor communication, invisibility, and insecurity in order to be the dependable, warrior-like father every black child needs.

*A nonresident father is* **not** *the same as an absent father.* One common assumption about the family structure is that a nonresident father is an absent father. This is certainly not true. An absent father is precisely that: *absent*. He is nowhere to be found. A nonresident father merely has a different home address than his children. He could very well be playing an integral role in the lives of his children, so visible that the only thing he doesn't do is sleep at his children's address. The truth about the single parent home is that the child has two parents, but only one lives in the home. We have to encourage nonresident fathers to take courage and assert their influence in their children's lives. We can never discount the role of the father who lives in another home.

*It's not just black boys who suffer.* As we discuss the need to build strong black men, we don't want to forget about building strong black women. Black girls need their fathers just as much as black boys do. Girls need to be able to see their father engaged in positive interactions with their mother. They need to see and experience their father treating women properly, which will help them understand how to evaluate young men in the dating process. They need their fathers to validate them, tell them they are beautiful, and treat them with respect so that they don't seek this affirmation in negative ways as they interact with the opposite sex.

*Social fathering: giving credit where credit is due.* We would like to salute one of the most overlooked categories in the realm of fatherhood. There aren't many statistics available on the countless grandfathers, uncles, stepfathers, significant others, teachers, coaches, and mentors that often fill the gaps left by biological fathers. We can't talk about fatherhood in the black community without considering the lasting impact that these special men have on the lives of young black men. Many of these men have biological children of their own but still make time to show love and support to young men who would otherwise be fatherless.

If you have the opportunity to teach, coach, or mentor a boy who does not have a father figure, please do not underestimate the power of your influence. Also, remember that it's not your sole responsibility to carry all the weight. Do what you can to make a difference in his life. If you are his teacher, do the best to invest in his education; if you are his coach, focus on teaching him the sport along with other virtues, such as sportsmanship. If you are his uncle, support him and be present as much as you can. It will take the collective efforts of his social fathering network. Take time to evaluate the role that you can play in his life.

## Blended Family Success

The reality is that black men don't always end up marrying or remaining married to the mother of their child. They, or the mother, often remarry after divorce or separation and create what is called the blended family. The blended family is complex but can be managed well when all adults involved consider what is best for the children involved. The downside of the blended family is that the children inevitably spend more time with the parent who was granted full custody. This allows them to bond more frequently, so the level of trust and affection for the parent who is present within the home increases. Another plus is that they can benefit from the love and support of additional family members.

In the twenty-first century, blended families are a reality. Regardless of the circumstances surrounding the inception of the blend, *all* parties involved in the child's life have to focus on raising a strong black man. If you are a stepfather, you have an influence on your stepson—especially in how you treat his mother. Treat his mother with respect and dignity. Remain cordial to his birth father if there is any contact, and set an example before him that he can model. You may not share his D.N.A, but you are an M.A.N. that he can look up to.

# ACTION STEPS

*Whether you live with your child or not, what specific steps do you need to take to be a present and involved father?*

*How will you overcome the challenges of being a fatherless father?*

*Are you satisfied with the legacy you are currently passing down to the next generation of young black men? If not, what legacy can you initiate that will bring pride for generations to come?*

# PART II

**What If I Can't Dribble, Dunk, Run Or Rap?**

**Let's Talk About Sex**

**Handle. Your. Business.**

# 4

# What If I Can't Dribble, Dunk, Run Or Rap?

*They might think they've got a pretty good jump shot or a pretty good flow, but our kids can't all aspire to be the next LeBron or Lil Wayne.*
*—President Barack Obama*

"I bet you can jump out of the gym." "I know you have rhythm, and I bet you can really sing." As a black man, I have heard those assumptions and others like them throughout my life. As black men we are a part of a legacy of great athletes, musicians, actors, and entertainers in a variety of genres. We also know that black men have and will continue to achieve greatness in many other professions beyond the worlds of sports and entertainment. It is encouraging and important for black boys to see black men on television who amaze them with their athletic or musical talent. It gives them something to aspire to become, and it gives them positive images and an ideal that inspires dreams. Therefore, it is important for us to reinforce to black boys the values of hard work both in the classroom and on the court. However, the majority of our young black men will "go pro" in something other than a sport or the field of entertainment. As we journey through this chapter, we will fully engage the title question above, as we continue to lay a foundation for the building of strong black men.

## The Player

My last year of college I was a resident adviser (RA) in a freshman coed dormitory. One of my residents was a young black man who stood about six feet three inches tall and looked athletic enough to have played virtually any sport he chose. On move-in day, the hallway bustled with activity, and students and their parents were everywhere. I walked up and down the hallway answering questions, giving directions, and helping move an occasional refrigerator or two.

As I moved about in the hall, I noticed that a group of students was gathered by the dorm room of my athletic-looking resident. Judging by the clamor, it felt a little like a celebrity had just entered our hall. As I moved closer, I understood what was happening. The group of students around his door was mostly young women. I am sure that there were a number of questions that he had been asked, but the one I heard loud and clear was "So, what did you *play* in high school?" probably assuming he played sports. "The saxophone." he said with slight annoyance in his tone. His response was clever, and I am sure it shocked everyone.

It turned out that this young man had obtained admission into the University of North Carolina at Greensboro School of Music, which was no less than extraordinary. While most prospective freshmen simply completed an admission application and awaited a reply, applicants to the School of Music had a much more arduous process. They had to apply for an audition and then perform in front of a group of professional and classically trained professors who listened to every tone and texture for the slightest flaw. Students in the music school spent over 60 percent of their college career in the music building, as we non-music students referred to it. The fact that this young man had the physique of an All-American but had the skill not only to play the saxophone, but also to play it well enough to make it into the music building, was most impressive.

Why is it that black men often have to fight the perception that we are athletic and enamored with hip-hop culture? It has a lot to do with our level of exposure. We as a society believe what we see, and the media often displays black men in the roles of athletes and entertainers. This consistent imagery can make it challenging to see black men as eclectic beings without vocational limitations. Why? Aside from media outlets and programming that specifically target the black community, we are all watching many of the same popular television stations, going to the same blockbuster movies, and visiting many of the same high-traffic websites. Within these media-built walls, the dominant perceptions about black men are formed.

It is important that we help our young men identify their innate talents and gifts. Those may be athletic, artistic, or in the areas of engineering, literature, or the sciences. The key is that we as parents, teachers, counselors, and mentors help nurture and cultivate those talents and gifts and not limit them based on perception.

## Like Mike ... If I Could Be Like Mike!

Who could forget the catchy jingle from the Gatorade commercials of the late 1990s? Michael Jordan, arguably the greatest basketball player of all time, had an endorsement deal with Gatorade, and the voice of the young man singing the jingle represented the voice of many young men of that era. When you ask young black men what they want to be when they grow up, you will often get one of two answers:

- NBA basketball player
- NFL football player

I was no exception. If you had talked to me in middle school and high school, you would have been convinced that I wanted to play basketball more than I wanted to breathe! I started young in elementary school and was on the right track. I worked on my game daily with relentless dedication. I practiced *before* practice and played year-round: on school teams in the winter, traveling teams in the spring, and at invitation-only camps during the summer. I was a pretty decent player in high school, had a high GPA along with the required SAT scores, and received recruiting interest from several college basketball programs. But even after my parents had spent thousands of dollars on sneakers, uniforms, equipment, and camp registrations, and I had spent countless hours in the gym in practice and games over the years, I didn't make it to the NBA. The reality for me was the same as it is for most young black men across the country that played high school basketball: the last game of our senior year is the last game of our competitive career. Now don't get me wrong. I would never tell a young black man that he *couldn't* do something. I certainly didn't let *anybody* tell me that!

Many young black men have been gifted by God with height, superior athletic ability, and what the athletic world calls a great sports IQ. All you have to do is watch a few games, and you will see that black men dominate the rosters of many professional basketball and football teams. For example, in 2013, black men represented 76.3 percent of the players on NBA teams. [13]

This is why it seems like a viable option to our young men today. If you're good enough, playing professional sports—particularly basketball and football—is a perfectly legal way to acquire wealth. But first you have to beat the odds.

## First Things First

Many young black men in middle and high school declare that they want to play in the NBA or NFL, yet they do not participate on their school team or *any*

---

13 The 2013 Racial And Gender Report Card: National Basketball Association; The Institute For Diversity And Ethics In Sport; http://www.tidesport.org/RGRC/2013/2013_NBA_RGRC.pdf (Retrieved on April 23, 2013).

organized team. This is nonsense. We are certainly in favor of going after your dreams, but the key words are *going after!* There are always a few exceptions, but the majority of the players on NBA and NFL teams played on their high school team and then received athletic scholarships and played college basketball or football at the Division I or II level. In the NBA, it is no longer possible to go straight from high school to the pros, as Kobe Bryant, Kevin Garnett, and LeBron James did. You must be talented enough to receive an athletic scholarship, and even if you're offered a scholarship and sign a national letter of intent, you must be academically eligible to play at that particular college or university. So, in order for you to be recognized by a college basketball coach or scout, you typically must first be a member of a high school team and probably an AAU (Amateur Athletic Union) team as well. College coaches don't go to random neighborhoods looking for pickup games in peoples' backyards or on neighborhood basketball courts to find their next star players. They attend high school games, AAU tournaments, and summer basketball camps to discover new talent. No pun intended, but you can't *score* if you're not in the game!

## NCAA College Sports

We must reiterate the fact that the majority of athletes that go on to play professional basketball or football are recipients of college athletic scholarships. Let's break it down with specifics: There are only thirteen total scholarships allowed for a Division I college basketball program each year. Division II college basketball programs are allowed a total of ten athletic scholarships. This means that, in a Division I school, if there are nine returning scholarship athletes from the previous season, there are only four scholarships available for the head coach to offer incoming freshmen and transfers for the next academic and athletic year.

For football, the numbers are much larger, as those teams require more players than basketball teams. However, the odds are not much better statistically. Division I football teams can offer eighty-five athletic scholarships for players, but again, because of returning players, each coach has a limited quantity available per year. Division II college football programs are allowed only thirty-six scholarships.[14] The number of high school players that have the skill, size, and aspiration to play college sports is easily in the tens of thousands. These players are vying for less than five thousand spots. There simply are not enough spots for the athletes that *are* good enough to play at the college level, let alone those that don't possess the necessary skill and ability.

We must be candid with young black men about the necessity of having a plan for successful living when their athletic careers are over. This applies both to the

14 Dave Galehouse, Varsityedge.com; http://www.varsityedge.com/nei/varsity.nsf/main/football+participation+numbers (Retrieved April 23, 2014).

potential McDonald's and Parade All-Americans as well as to those who will never capture the attention of a college athletic program.

## The NBA

Let's say you are parenting or mentoring a young black man who has the skill and size to play at the college level. He signs a scholarship and plays four years and has a realistic chance to play professionally. Even if he is one of the best players at the college level, there are still numbers to face when he finishes college. The annual NBA draft has only two rounds to select a total of sixty eligible players, and each team is limited to a few picks each round. There are only thirty NBA teams with a maximum of twelve roster spots on each team.[15] There are a maximum of 360 NBA players at any given time. It is also important to note that these 360 players include both veteran players and rookies (first-year players). So if a team has twelve players at the conclusion of the season prior to the draft, and they select two more new players, one in each round of the draft, how do they keep from being fined by the league for exceeding the team roster maximum? If you assumed that at least two of the players are cut or released from the team, you assumed correctly.

## The NFL

There are thirty-two teams in the National Football League. The annual NFL draft has seven rounds, and there are thirty-two picks (one pick for each team) per round. This suggests that 224 players are selected each year. However, as in the case of the NBA, many of these players will have to earn their spots competing against returning veteran players during training camp. There is a maximum of fifty-three roster spots on a pro team, so that means there are 1,696 NFL players employed at any given time. Again, this number includes veteran players and rookies.

It's been estimated that the average career tenure of a player that makes it to the NFL, which many say should stand for "Not For Long", is three years. This means that most players that get drafted after their senior year in college, assuming they are at least twenty-two years old, will probably be officially retired from the game of football forever at the young, tender age of twenty-five. In other words, even if you are one of the fortunate few that make it to the pros, the reality is that you will spend the majority of your adult life making a living from something other than being an NFL player.

---

15 The National Basketball Association, http://www.nba.com/analysis/00421026.html) (Retrieved December 14, 2014).

## Tough Love

We *must* care enough to level with our young men and inform them that if they are not serious enough to dedicate themselves to put in the hard work and sacrifice, the goal of playing college—let alone pro—sports is not realistic for them. This is *tight* but it's right! You will help them a lot more by being honest with them about the numbers and helping them to develop a plan to execute when their playing days are over, regardless of whether they play their last game on their high school's field or inside an NFL stadium. Believe me, they will appreciate you for it in the long run.

## Shoot for the Moon

We are not saying that a young man should not aspire to be a professional athlete. However, we do want to be clear about the demands and costs involved in reaching such an elite level. Becoming professionally proficient in *anything* requires education, training, and dedication. Let young black men know that doing the least will produce the least. No one achieves success overnight and without sacrifice. You can't *be* something without first *becoming* it. Every professional *becomes* a member of his desired profession through years of obtaining the proper education, networking, and professional development and training. You cannot reach proficiency, let alone mastery, in any field without dedication.

Professional athletics is an excellent goal because imitating your favorite athlete on the field or court requires other virtues and disciplines that have utility for life in general. For example, working to become the next LeBron James or Adrian Peterson will require that you attend and do well in school, practice, work out, and, if you have any time and energy left, eat and sleep. Then you do it all over again the next day. The point is to encourage our young men to participate in competitive athletics and other extracurricular activities. The very nature of competition requires that you follow rules, work cooperatively with a team, and demonstrate good sportsmanship.

When my mother registered me for Little League baseball, her intent was not that I go pro and make millions of dollars, though I am sure she would not have been disappointed if I had. Her intent was to expose me to coaches who could be positive male figures and teach me the values associated with organized sports. I still remember the Little League pledge that we recited before every game. The end of that pledge stated, "I will play fair and strive to win, but win or lose, I will always do my best." Even though I did not make the big leagues, play college baseball, or even make my high school team, just walking away from my Little League experience with the value to always do my best was a major lesson my mother wanted me to learn. We should use athletics and other forms of recreational activities as tools and resources to build good character and to help motivate our young men to aspire to fulfill their potential. Not all lessons have to be learned in one-on-one mentoring sessions or afterschool programs. Young black men can and will learn many valuable lessons via competitive sports and other extracurricular activities of their choice. Inform them that the purpose of their participation is to develop an understanding of leadership, teamwork, perseverance, and the ability to bounce back from failure or defeat, which will serve them well for the remainder of their lives.

There is no excuse for young black men being unaware of career options outside of sports and entertainment. Some of them may be gifted in athletics or the arts, and in this case they should be encouraged to pursue their chosen field with diligence. They should also be informed that there are many behind-the-scenes occupations in sports and entertainment that may be a perfect fit for them. Unfortunately, the majority of the media's footage shows only the athletes and entertainers living lives of prosperity. More attention should be given to the types of jobs in these fields that provide better odds and are less volatile on a young man's ability to establish and maintain a consistent income. Careers in sports management, where the agent representing the athlete receives 10 to 20 percent of the value of the deals they negotiate, are often overlooked but are extremely necessary to the visibility and profitability of world-class athletes like LeBron James, Kobe Bryant, Julius Peppers, and Tiger Woods. Organizations like the Black Sports Agents Association (BSAA), cofounded by the Reverend Jesse Jackson, provide information on the tremendous opportunity in this field and the steps to take to be successful. Remember that behind every Jay-Z or Lil Wayne is a manager, publicist, and fashion stylist who helps to sustain his image and constant presence in the media.

As models for these young men, we must be diligent to present them with the many opportunities that their exposure and vision prevents them from seeing. Many of our young black men can quickly list the names of today's biggest hip-hop stars featured on the BET Awards. However, many of these same young men have no knowledge of the story of Robert "Bob" Johnson, who founded Black Entertainment Television (BET Networks) and helped to create the programming that allowed us to learn more about the lives of these entertainers. We also need to share with our young black men that this same Mr. Johnson, though he never played college or professional basketball, was a co-owner of the NBA's Charlotte Bobcats (now known as the Charlotte Hornets) along with Michael Jordan.

## I'm Gonna Buy That Boy a Watermelon!

As I mentioned earlier, my mother signed me up for Little League baseball when I was in the second grade as a way to expose me to positive male figures. I was a fast runner, relative to my peers. On one particular occasion, I remember hitting the ball off the tee and running as fast as I could. I will admit, it felt good to hear people cheering as I rounded the bases. Everything was great until a woman in the crowd said to my mother, "I'm gonna buy that boy a watermelon!" I did not hear the comment or even understand it as I heard my mother explain the situation to my aunts. I did understand by the tone and volume in her voice that she was angry. The woman, who was white, saw a black boy who could run fast and help his team win the game. The perception my mother wanted to avoid was that her little black son was loved and praised only when he hit home runs and performed well in sports. She responded to the woman's stereotypical remark by saying, "No thank you, we will take him out for pizza later."

I was a decent baseball player, but I always had the awareness that my professional career would include something other than playing a pro sport. My career has exposed me to young men who have bought into the idea that the only way they can legitimately *make it* out of their dire living situations is to excel in sports, music, or some form of entertainment. Many of them do not take school seriously or have given up on school all together. They have believed the lie that they are not intelligent or academically inclined. So they have let their academic success fall by the wayside in the hopes of getting that watermelon or some reward for their ability to entertain.

The odds of a young man getting into college are much greater than him getting into the NBA or NFL. As leaders in the lives of young black men, we have to recalibrate the hype by focusing on business, political, and literary icons—some renowned, and many more previously unknown. We suggest that your mentoring initiatives include heavy emphasis on the lifestyles of local, upstanding black men in your communities. These strong black men will share their success stories face-to-face and provide opportunities for young men to establish real-world connections and build networks. They don't need to be rich or famous. They simply need to be willing to share.

We have to heighten the awareness of the many career paths young black men can pursue to make the money and enjoy the lifestyle they want. We can't wait for the schools or media to highlight the accomplishments of black professionals or entrepreneurs. If we want to expose them to successes in the black community, we have to do it. We must seek out job coaches, career counselors, and the talented writers, producers, and videographers within our communities and networks, pooling resources if necessary, to create high-quality programming that is competitive with what is force-fed to our young black men. This programming should feature the countless untold stories of successful black professionals and entrepreneurs who are living well as a result of the value they bring to society.

Black athletes and entertainers are only a small fraction of the black male population. Because they are in the forefront, they are more visible, and their lives look like something to aspire to. But there are far more black doctors, plumbers, counselors, teachers, and carpenters than black entertainers. In chapter 6, we will identify many of the career options available outside of the sports and entertainment realm. Now let's examine another sector of the entertainment industry that is particularly enticing to our young black men.

## The Next Kendrick Lamar or Lil Wayne?

*Maybe you are the next Lil Wayne, but probably not, in which case you need to stay in school.*
—*President Barack Obama*

These words were famously spoken by President Barack Obama who used the successful rapper's career as an example of what most young black men will not accomplish in the music industry. Why would he say something that most would consider heartless? Here are two reasons why:

1.  There are far too many black boys expressing desires to be NBA, NFL, or hip-hop stars. We need more who are publicly aspiring to gain careers as educators, engineers, doctors, and entrepreneurs.
2.  The music business is a *business*. Talent and good looks alone are not enough to keep you relevant. There are many *talented* people in the world. You must learn the business in order to have a legitimate shot at success.

Communicate the true purpose of the media to young black men in your care so that they will not be so easily manipulated by what they see on the big screen. The media was designed to communicate messages of urgency and relevance to a massive audience as consistently as possible. Newsworthy content often is limited to celebrity coverage, fear-inducing imagery, and political commentary.

## The Real Music Industry

The music business is a business. Businesses exist to make money from the sale of products, and the objective of the music industry is to sell records. Period. If you are an artist signed to a record deal and your music doesn't make the label money, you will probably lose your spot on the label's artist roster. There were many "one-hit wonders" that prove this point! The lifestyles and imagery presented to our young black men are not the reality for many in the recording industry.

In today's music industry, recording artists are being offered 360 deals: contracts that allow a record label to receive a percentage of the earnings from all of an artist or band's activities rather than just record sales. In the past, artists were signed to the more traditional record deals and received an advance when they signed a contract. An advance is basically a loan against their future earnings from sales of their album. Unless they sell enough copies (and for some this literally means *millions)* of their album, their royalty statements will show a negative balance—meaning they actually owe the record label money. Record royalties for artists are not payable until the advance or loan has been "recouped" or repaid to the record label. For example, the record label pays for things such as the rental fees for the mansions, expensive cars, and jewelry featured in music videos. These are all considered recoupable expenses. Basically, this means many artists are not making money from their record deals. This is why they must tour, attempt to secure gigs, act, do product endorsements, and appear in reality TV shows. These opportunities are usually available only to the most successful and recognizable artists.

If you or a young black man you know is aspiring to music industry success, we highly recommend reading books such as James Walker's *This Business of Urban Music*, which includes information specific to the music industry at large as well as for those pursuing the genres of R&B, hip-hop, and gospel. A few more books that will increase your understanding are Donald Passman's *All You Need to Know about the Music Business* and Kashif's *Everything You Need to Know about the Record Industry*. In other words, encourage the young men under your tutelage to read anything they can get their hands on in order to gain more knowledge about the business of music, if this is what they truly desire to do.

## Don't Believe the Hype

There is a difference between facts and truth. Below are a few common perceptions and the corresponding realities for those experiencing music industry success.

**Perception:** Hip-hop artists keep it real and are true to the lifestyles featured in the videos on television and YouTube.
**Reality**: Reread the section above on the realities for many recording artists. Most successful rappers, singers, and entertainers no longer feel safe living in the crime-ridden and violent neighborhoods they describe in their music.

**Perception:** Hip-hop artists are hustlers who sell drugs as a part of their hustle.
**Reality**: The most successful rappers don't sell drugs. It's too risky, because they keep a high profile and they have too much to lose. Their income is generated from recording and publishing deal advances, royalties, touring revenue, businesses, and endorsement deals.

**Perception:** Hip-hop artists have multiple women, just like they rap about in their videos.
**Reality**: Many of them are not bachelors and "playas" but are in committed relationships with one woman or are married men with families. Many of the women featured in videos do not know the artists personally, auditioned for the roles they played, and were considered "hired help".

**Perception:** Hip-hop artists and singers make a lot of money and live in huge mansions.

**Reality**: The majority of rappers and singers are not rich and don't make any more money than most adults who work full-time jobs. Fame and wealth are *not* the same. There are many famous people in the entertainment industry that are struggling financially.

## Is Hip Hop to Blame?

Some hip-hop music, through lyrics and videos, suggest that black males are primarily interested in hustling, making money, pimping women, and bling. Many have wondered if it's possible that a single genre of music is destroying our young black men. We personally do not think that hip-hop is solely responsible, because it would take a lot more than a musical style to destroy and divide a race or group of people. A better question to ponder is "Does hip-hop have a negative impact on the lives of young black men?"

I am not a frequent consumer of controversial news-driven talk shows, but one particular interview held my attention. On the Fox News program the O'Reilly Factor, Bill O'Reilly hosted a discussion between recording artist Cam'ron, producer Damon Dash, and a middle school principal. The dialogue focused on how some of Cam'ron's lyrics were derogatory and promoted negative images that young people try to emulate. The discussion took a turn when the principal sought to hold Cam'ron and other artists responsible for having a negative influence on the lives and minds of young people. The recording artist ignited a fiery exchange when he asserted that parents are responsible to influence the behavior of their own children. He urged the principal to hold more parent-teacher conferences and seek to have a more positive influence on their youth. The principal then insisted that Cam'ron and other hip-hop artists have great influence on children from single-parent homes. He explained that many of his students did not have positive home environments to help buffer the negativity coming from the lyrics of hip-hop artists. Damon Dash interjected that if the young people listening to Cam'ron really emulated him, they would be entrepreneurs, possess business acumen, and enjoy corporate success.

What concerned me most about the discussion was that the finger was pointed and the blame shifted from the hip-hop industry to the parents and back again. Each side could have cited countless examples to support their views. When we fight over who is to blame, we waste valuable time and energy that could be spent on creating solutions. In truth, we are *collectively* responsible for our young men.

The dialogue between Cam'ron and the principal mirrored many discussions that I have been privy to over the years. But our focus is on what we can do to *stop blaming each other* and *start working with each other* to build our young men. It would have been a delight to see Cam'ron and the principal converge their intensity and energy into a brainstorming session that would have been broadcast to the thousands of viewers watching the program.

Hip-hop has been, and continues to be, a contentious and divisive subject in the United States. On one hand, we adore hip-hop as an art form and a means of creative expression and artistry. On the other hand, we abhor how it is often used as a platform to express violence, to spew obscenities, and to degrade black women. The participants in the discussion said that hip-hop is merely an expression of the ills that are inherent in American society in general.

Other participants spoke about the evolution of hip-hop as an art form and pointed out that it is a popular genre in the white community as well. Others discussed the double standard in that white America can produce pornography, but when the hip-hop industry produces a music video with images of *nearly* naked women, it creates outrage. The debate also included the economic exploitation of the genre and highlighted the hypocrisies and atrocities produced by the genre. *Hip-Hop vs. America* was simply a well-crafted and well-articulated debate that left my thoughts provoked but offered few tangible solutions. So once again, we were left with much to think about, but even more to do.

As we think about building strong black men, we have to ask ourselves one key question: why has hip-hop had such a profound impact? More specifically, why has its influence been so pronounced in the black community? Our aim is not to indict hip-hop or the entertainment industry but to acknowledge the impact all forms of entertainment have on the psyches of our young men.

In my counseling practice, I spend most of my time building rapport and seeking to understand my clients first. I work to ascribe causality to their behavior after developing some measure of trust. In seeking to understand and best serve my clients, I would be misguided to ignore the power and lure of music, especially hip-hop, which is a common point of reference for many of my clients. I often ask who their favorite artists are and then ask them to describe why they like those particular artists. Their answers routinely revolve around a consistent core: getting money, keeping it real, going hard, and getting with girls. Successful presentations tend to inspire and ignite action. Hip-hop presents an image, a means, and a platform of getting some very real and legitimate needs met. Let's look at each of the components mentioned, which will give us a little more insight to the psyche of young men and help us understand why hip-hop has such an impact.

**Getting money.** Young men simply want what many of us want: money to provide a means of living a secure and comfortable lifestyle. Hip-hop offers an illusion of grandeur and economic freedom. Though we know they are illusions, we cannot deny that illusions and mirages look good at first glance. We have to help our young men see how those artists really make their money and how the business really works. For example, when I worked for a youth development center, I invited guest speakers who had experience working in the entertainment industry to provide an inside look at the realities of hip-hop and the music industry. The speakers were able to explain, as we did earlier in this chapter, the realities of *getting money*.

*Keeping it real.* Young men, particularly those who have experienced some type of trauma, such as the abandonment of one or both parents or being passed around from program to program, will not talk to you unless you are authentic. If they do talk to you, their conversation will not move below the surface. They have to know that you are trustworthy, and one of the best ways to build trust is to be open and honest with them from the very beginning. They can see when you are not being yourself and not relating to them from a place of authenticity. Hip-hop's artists often shoot straight with their lyrics, call it how they see it, and use clear and direct communication, even if it is not always positive. Young men are drawn to that level of communication, and we have to be equally as real and genuine when working with them. They need a platform that fosters authentic expression. We can organize panel discussions, open-mics, forums, and group think tanks where they can assemble regularly. Such outlets provide an opportunity to voice their dreams as well as their frustrations. We can't help them get what they want in a positive and constructive manner if we don't know their story and what motivates them.

*Going hard.* It appears that hip-hop artists are uninhibited and say and do anything they want to, with no regard for consequences. Often young men talk about some of their exploits in my sessions. Many times they exaggerate, if not blatantly lie. Their fundamental desire is to have something to aspire to and something to work toward. As parents, practitioners, and concerned adults, we have to set the standard for the pursuit of purpose and what is noble for a young man to aspire to. Otherwise life's most salient lessons will continue to be taught by those that appear to be going hard and living life to its fullest. We must define for them what it means to give your all to something and help build opportunities for a better, brighter tomorrow.

*Getting the girls.* The objectification of women through both the words and images in some hip-hop music and videos is a point of debate. Amid the sensationalized and often degrading depictions of women in hip-hop, we miss what young men really long for. They want relational intimacy, which all people want. In today's mainstream hip-hop, the artists consistently talk about women in terms of volume. It is typical to hear them boasting about the number of women they have. Volume of women voids intimacy with women. Intimacy is built via time, intensity, and a depth of relationship. It is common for teen fathers to brag about the number of girls they had, even while with the mother of their child. However, in a one-on-one session, they are quick to lament how they wish they could have a better relationship with their child's mother. The longing is there, but we have to bring it out and set the example for how to build healthy relationships.

## Where Do We Go from Here?

Whether you love it or hate it, hip-hop is an art form that is here to stay. Similarly, the glorification of sports and athletes has no expiration date. Obviously, they both have pros and cons, just like many other influential elements of popular culture. Our role as builders is to educate our young men and to set the example so that they have a way to temper what they see and hear. It is our collective job to define for them what is real and how to get their needs met in legitimate ways.

# ACTION STEPS

*What will you do to help young black men understand that they are not limited to careers in sports and entertainment?*

*How can you assist young black men in discovering their gifts and talents?*

*How can you help young black men see hip hop as a form of entertainment rather than a life style to aspire to?*

# 5
# Let's Talk About Sex

*A woman brought you into this world so you have no right to disrespect one.*
— *Tupac Shakur*

I fondly remember the first time I made the two-hour drive to Granville County, North Carolina, to meet my wife's family. We were both in college, and it was the Christmas holiday season. It's always a major ordeal to meet a girl's parents for the first time, but being invited over for a Christmas dinner is on a totally different level when it comes to making a good first impression. Since it was a family gathering, I knew that I would meet her parents and possibly her sister and older brothers. However, I was in for a surprise when I arrived at the address she gave me.

I began to slow down as I got closer to the neighboring homes and noticed the staggering number of vehicles parked along the street. It seemed that the endless line of cars was connected to the house she described. I wondered if I had the right address. I realized a small, intimate evening with immediate family might have just turned into a festive extended family and friends celebration with me on the hot seat. I parked and began making my way to the front door. With each step, I considered everything from my attire, to the level of firmness of my handshake, to the friendliness of my smile and demeanor. I pondered potential answers to questions such as:

"So, tell me about yourself and your family."

"What are your intentions with my daughter?"

"What are your plans after college?"

"Do you have a job?"

"What are your interests?"

I thought about not only what type of guy my future wife expected me to be but also what type her parents, siblings, and extended family expected me to be. I was sure they knew I was coming and they were ready for me. All that mattered at that point was that I was ready to meet them too.

I rang the doorbell, and sure enough, there appeared to be at least twenty-five people there. When she mentioned she came from a large family, she wasn't exaggerating! I had heard horror stories before from other guys who had met the parents and family of a girlfriend for the first time in situations like this. Fortunately, I had a great experience meeting her family that night. Numerous people asked me numerous questions. Apparently I gave the right answers, because we continued to date, and ultimately her family became my family. I believed the best person I could possibly be in that situation was my true, authentic self. I knew that there was no way I could go wrong doing that.

I was able to stand up in a high-pressure situation, but not all young men would have fared as well. I needed certain characteristics. With many eyes watching, someone would have detected if I were faking it to make it. It is important to note that a young man's greatest asset is to be secure within himself, and those qualities will be evident in a variety of situations.

Having the proper perspective regarding the opposite sex is not just about appearing to be a gentleman. It is about *being* a gentleman. It is about being the same guy at the family Christmas party as you are with the fellas in the locker room. It is not about being a patient wolf lying in wait for the right moment to strike. It is about respecting the young woman you are with, even when there are no eyes watching. It is understanding the game and learning to play by the rules.

## The Dating Game

Your value is not based on how many numbers you can get, how many dates you have, or how many girls you have sex with. If she gave you her number that easily, she is probably just that easy. If you go to a party, club, or the local Wal-Mart and get a girl's number after talking to her for a few moments—or even worse, after shouting something like "Hey, shorty," or "What up, ma"—it really does not mean that your talk game is all that tight as much as it means she may be just that loose! Don't play yourself. Ten other guys probably have the same number.

Dating is not a platform of conquest to see how many girls you can sleep with. The dating game, like other games, can be fun, can provide a platform for learning, and can cultivate responsibility and maturity. For dating to produce the best result, it is important to have guidelines and boundaries and to stay within them. Dating is important for multiple reasons, and here are some of the benefits of playing the dating game by the rules:

*Your value is not based on how many numbers you can get, how many dates you have, or how many girls you have sex with.*

**Build confidence**. It takes courage to ask someone on a date, because she always has the potential to reject you. You will hear the word *no* throughout your life, so learning to accept it and move forward has value for other aspects of life. You cannot control the answer; you can control whether or not you ask.

**Cultivate creativity.** Dating is an excellent time to create a fun environment that both people will enjoy. Dinner and a movie is fine, but thinking outside of the box and doing something different is even better. If you don't think you are the most creative person, ask for advice from others and search the Internet for creative ideas.

**Selflessness.** Dating gives you a chance to have fun while you are learning about someone else's personality, likes, dislikes, and interests. When on a date, use it as a time to get to know her by asking questions and really listening to the answers. It is not always about you.

**Enhance social skills.** Dates often take place in public settings, such as restaurants, amusement parks, museums, movie theaters, or concert arenas. Thus you have to learn to interact with your date and other individuals in the context of a social situation. Dating gives you the chance to use and enhance your communication skills as you talk with waiters and waitresses and other individuals.

How should you act on a date and how should you treat the young woman? I often hear young men say that girls these days really don't respect themselves; then they ask me why they should show respect. My answer: maybe the young woman will begin to respect herself if you treat her respectfully. Even if she does not, you still have no right to disrespect her. When I talk to young men about treating girls the way they would want a guy to treat their own sister, they always argue or laugh and say, "Nah, that's different." Young men, ask yourself this question: "Would I want some dude treating my sister the way I treat other young women?" If the answer is no, you need to change the way you are treating the opposite sex.

## Real-Talk about Relationships

Several years ago, a former principal asked me to create a character education course. Knowing that teenagers have an opinion on *everything*, I decided to make in-class discussions a portion of their grade for the class. This would make the course more interesting and allow the students to vent and to discuss topics that they would never cover in any of their core classes.

On discussion days, the students eagerly scribbled their anonymous questions in all capital letters to conceal their identity and dropped them in a bucket for me to shake and draw randomly. I found that many of the questions sought advice on dating and relationships. I was known as Mr. R by many of the students, so as a tribute to my male students, who were always curious about how to connect with the ladies, I would like to share some of the Q&A content to help guide some of your potential discussions with young black men.

> **Q: How can I get more girls?**
> A: Stop *trying* to get more girls.
> **Q: I've got sports, school, and family stuff to do, but my girl wants me to spend more time with her? How do I deal with this?**
> A: If you're not married, don't act like it.
> **Q: I started calling this girl after she gave me her number, but all of a sudden she stopped returning my calls. What's up with that?**
> A: Girls like to be pursued, not stalked.
> **Q: I've got a date with this girl, and I want to make sure it goes right. What should I do?**
> A: Treat her the way you'd want another man to treat your mom or sister.
> **Q: My girlfriend told me that if I go to college out of state, we probably won't work out. What do you think?**
> A: She's probably right. Ask her what her goals are aside from being in a relationship with you. If she doesn't have any, move on.

There is already a considerable amount of information out there on how to impress the ladies and figure out what they are looking for. We wrote this book to speak life and wisdom into the lives of young black men and to offer solutions to those working with them. Instead of adding to the extensive *how to get the ladies* list, below we'd like to alert young brothers to some of the pitfalls to look out for when dealing with the opposite sex.

## You Probably Shouldn't Be with Her If:

*She wants a "bad boy" or a thug.* Never change who you are for someone else. If you're so busy trying to be like somebody else, who will ever get to know the real you? Besides, if you change, she may decide she doesn't like the "new you" either. It's always best to be yourself. You can never mess that up. I don't care how pretty she is, if she's not smart enough to value you for speaking politely, opening a door for her, respecting her body, having good grades, and valuing yourself and your personal goals, then *leave her alone.* Don't play the fool and try to act like a thug when you're not. There's no real future in *thuggin'* anyway.

***She only wants you for your money.*** If you have to continually buy things for her to be happy, she's not the one. She's using you for material purposes. If she says the relationship will be over or she starts acting funny the minute you can't afford something or choose not to buy it for her, you know something is wrong. Gentlemen, we must be smarter than this, no matter how *fine* she is. It is important for a man to be able to provide money, but you're not obligated to do this until you "put a ring on it." A good woman loves you for you, not for what you can do for her.

***She wants to date other guys while dating you.*** You may not be married, but it's important to make sure you set boundaries on this one, especially if *she* has issues with *you* seeing someone else in addition to her. That's called a double standard. A man wants a woman who is just as committed to the relationship as he is. Seeing multiple people at the same time is complicated and usually is not a good thing. If this is a necessity for her, maybe you should just be friends.

***She doesn't have goals.*** At a certain age, this is okay. But we are living in the twenty-first century. In this era, people in their teens are starting businesses online every day, learning skills like software programming in elementary and middle school, creating the next major video games and the next major social networks, and volunteering to gain experience in various fields prior to attending college. The college admissions process is getting more competitive every year, and college costs are more expensive than ever before. Girls have been known to mature faster than boys, so her lack of goals might be a red flag, especially if you are clear about your goals and what you want to accomplish in life. Once you turn eighteen, you will be making adult decisions for the rest of your life. If you don't have a specific destination, it really doesn't matter what road you take and who you ride with. Think about that for minute. There will be plenty of time for girls. You can't do much for a female prior to adulthood without an income anyway. Get yourself together, make your own plans, and pursue your dream. If she's truly the one for you, your dreams and goals won't run her away.

Dating and showing interest in the opposite sex is natural for young men and usually creates opportunities for intimacy and sexual activity. Therefore, it is important for mature men to engage them in healthy conversations about sex.

## Let's Talk about Sex

When it comes to sex, the very best thing we can do for our young men is talk about it. At what age should we start talking to our young men about girls, dating, and sex? Talk about it often and as early as the elementary school years. Why? Given the ease of access to the Internet and other forms of media, sexual imagery is more available than ever. It is not uncommon for elementary-age children to be exposed to songs, videos, and movies (even cartoons) that have sexual references. It is best for parents or adults to help interpret these images and ideas and to provide a context for younger children.

It may not be necessary to expound in detail, but it is important to at least begin to engage with children over the idea of sex while they are young. Often sex is dealt with in terms of extremes: it is treated either as a shameful act that is to be avoided and kept secret or as a sensationalized act that is flaunted and displayed without shame. Sex is a natural part of life and should be discussed as our children grow up. The sex talk is not a one-time lecture that we have once they reach puberty, but an ongoing conversation that we have with them throughout their lives.

As we have mentioned, boys learn a lot by observing. They notice what we say to them about women, and they take careful note of how we treat the opposite sex. We can tell them to treat women with respect, but they have to *see* us modeling respectful treatment toward women. The sex talk is instilled over time and is mostly about how to view yourself and the opposite sex with respect and dignity. Boys will see an abundance of distorted examples in the media and through cyberspace of how to view the opposite sex. Again, your involvement does not have to be the intense "birds and bees talk" but rather it can be something as simple as checking a young man if he sees an attractive young woman at a shopping mall and makes a derogatory comment. It is about capturing the teachable moments that present themselves.

Current research has dispelled the myth that men think about sex eight thousand times per day (every seven seconds); it has been found to be closer to twenty times per day.[16] The same research suggests that the older a man becomes, the less he thinks about the act of sex. How much more do you think a teenage boy who is experiencing puberty thinks about sex? Whether we want to admit it or not, some kids *are* having sex in one form or another by the time they reach middle school.

We can try to scare them straight all we want, but it won't work for the majority. Everywhere they look, from television to movies to magazine stands to the Internet, sex is suggested loud and clear. Youth aren't as naïve as you may think. They already know that sex doesn't always result in pregnancy or sexually transmitted diseases. Instead of attempting to communicate fear, talk to them about their potential, their dreams, and their future aspirations. Talk to them about their personal value and self-worth. Those of us who counsel, teach, parent, and mentor young men need to remind them that their worth is not based on how many young women they have sex with.

We need to show and tell young men that sex and self-worth are two different things. We must educate them on the purpose of sex and encourage them to build relationships that are not based on sex but on mutual respect. Rather than live in denial, it would be a lot easier to be straight up with our young men, level with

---

16 Emily Caldwell, Study debunks stereotype that men think about sex all day long Ohio State University, news release, Nov. 29, 2011; http://news.osu.edu/search.html?search=New+Study+Debunks&id=27 (May 3, 2012).

them, and let them know that we live in the twenty-first century too. If you're not talking to them about sex, somebody else is.

Of course, there is nothing wrong with young men talking to young women, hanging out, and having a good time, but the rush to have sex has led to an overabundance of teen parents, fatherless homes, and a myriad of emotional, mental, and health problems. It is good for us as fathers, teachers, coaches, counselors, and mentors to discuss this subject, because we really have been there and done that. Otherwise, they will end up taking their cues about sex from peers who may be taking their cues from the Internet, television, radio, or other media. We live in a society and culture that is full of sex, so we should provide the buffer. Don't fear putting an idea about sex in their heads. It is likely already there, and it is likely to grow more misguided and distorted without guidance. It is better that they have this conversation with us rather than with their "boys" in the locker room, who are perhaps just as lost, confused, and misguided.

One of my most memorable clients was a young man who conceived his son at the age of thirteen; he turned fourteen just before his son's birth. He was referred to me for parenting skills and to participate in a group that I offered for young fathers. As I counseled him on his newly acquired responsibilities, I realized that this young man could not do anything necessary to take care of his child; he could hardly take care of himself. So I refrained from the "take care of your responsibilities, young man" talk. What was he going to do, get a job? No, because a fourteen-year-old is not of legal age to work. So this young man could not pay child support even if he wanted to. The best way to take care of his responsibility was to take care of himself. I encouraged him to focus on the tangible and immediate influence he could have in his son's life by doing the seemingly small things, like talking to his son, holding him, and reading to him. I stressed the importance of self-care and working to better himself so that one day he could be the material, financial, and emotional provider his son needed. The real responsibility falls on us men. We are *on the hook* to talk to our young men and provide productive options before, not after, they become fourteen-year-old fathers.

## Safe Sex in the Twenty-First Century

It is not uncommon to hear the phrase "safe sex" in a variety of contexts. Often the discussion of safe sex ranges from the use of protection to abstaining altogether. It is important to note that abstinence is *safe* but it is *not* sex, and using protection is sex, but it is not 100 percent safe. Having safe sex that is both safe and sex requires the following steps:

- Abstain from *all* forms of sexual activity.
- Enter a relationship with a partner who has also abstained from *all* forms of sexual activity.
- Engage in sexual activity only with that person.
- Engage in sex with that person for the rest of your life.

Abstinence followed by monogamous sex with a partner who has also been abstinent is the only way to have sex that is guaranteed to be safe. The abstinence-followed-by-monogamy idea may sound like pure idealism, but there are young people who have devoted themselves to remaining abstinent until they enter a committed marriage relationship. In fact, when I worked in college ministry, many of the students I counseled and advised desired to remain abstinent until marriage. I also remember having counseling sessions with them after they were not able to uphold their commitment and were dealing with feelings of guilt and regret. They often told me that "one thing led to another," and before they knew it they had either gone too far or gone all the way.

> *A condom may protect a young man from an unwanted pregnancy, AIDS, or an STD, but what protects him from the emotional and psychological dangers? We do not focus enough on the mental and emotional damage that occurs when a boy engages in sex before he is emotionally mature enough.*

An important point to note is that the value of abstaining until marriage or until a relational commitment is made still exists in our culture. However, we have to face the fact that, as a whole, young men today are going to have sex and are not going to remain in monogamous relationships. In fact, the Centers for Disease Control disclosed in a 2011 report that the percentage of black teen males who reported ever having sex was 72 percent, which is greater than that of Hispanics (53 percent) and whites (40 percent).[17] Even if the data is skewed due to hyperbole, ego-tripping, or just plain lies, the fact that black male teens found it necessary to *lie* about their sexual activity is still cause for concern.

If boys don't hear phrases from men such as "sex does not make you a man," "it is okay if you don't want to have sex," "being a virgin is nothing to be ashamed of," and "sex is worth the wait," they may feel the need to lie about their sexual behavior. They may fall prey to lies and the skewed idea that something is wrong with them if they are not sexually active. Even if 72 percent of black teen males are not sexually active, we know many are. If we cannot stop a behavior, we can manage it and mitigate the potential for destructive consequences. For example, research in the world of addiction science is clear that the longer you keep a child from experimenting with and using drugs, the less likely it is that he will develop a

---

17 The Centers for Disease Control and Prevention http://www.cdc.gov/media/releases/2011/P0405_vitalsigns.html[12] ( Retrieved October 5, 2012).

drug abuse or addiction problem.[18] This is true for any behavior. Sex is a wonderful way to express love, and it is full of benefits, but for the teenage male, whose brain and body is not yet fully developed, it could cause an array of problems.

Of course, the obvious problems are physical consequences such as the human immunodeficiency virus (HIV), acquired immune deficiency syndrome (AIDS), sexually transmitted diseases (STDs), and sexually transmitted infections (STIs). However, we often fail to acknowledge the mental and emotional consequences. A condom may protect a young man from an unwanted pregnancy, AIDS, or an STD, but what protects him from the emotional and psychological dangers? We do not focus enough on the mental and emotional damage that occurs when a boy engages in sex before he is emotionally mature enough.

In one of my teen father groups, a young man admitted that he almost cried the first time he had sex. He explained that he had never experienced anything that felt that good in his life. He was hooked! Needless to say, he became driven to have sex and began to realize that it was an urge that he could have satisfied by different women. He lost his innocence and was not emotionally prepared to control himself. It did not take long before he was having sex without even using a condom. The result was conception at the age of fifteen.

Sexually active young men begin to lose reverence for women, and they also lose restraint. Because their brains are not fully developed, they have a limited ability to control their impulses. It is like they have the keys to a high-performance sports car without ever having had driving lessons. Instead of him driving his impulses, his impulses are driving him, and often they are driving him too far and way too fast.

Sex is best expressed in relationships where both people are stable and mature enough to handle the physical, mental, and emotional intensity. Given the gravity of teen sexual behavior and the potential for harm, what do we say to our young men to help them navigate this very real and sometimes complicated life situation? Young men tend to resist blanket statements like "stay drug free", "wait until you get married to have sex", and "if someone hits you, walk away". Let's face reality: in the heat of any moment—whether it is the temptation to use drugs, have sex, or bust somebody in the mouth—it is tough to think clearly. If we are going to help our young men avoid the pitfalls of premature or premarital sex, we have to offer viable options. Here is how we can help:

***Form all-male groups and educate young men about the changes occurring in their bodies.*** Sex education classes are helpful, but young men also need a forum that allows candid questions and answers from a male perspective.

***Explain that what they are feeling is normal.*** Sex presents the great dilemma of being both wonderful and potentially destructive. Let's take away the stigma by telling them it is okay to feel sexual desire, and then provide wise counsel on how to contain those desires.

---

18 Anthony JC, Petronius KR. Early-onset drug use and risk of later drug problems. Drug and Alcohol Dependence. Drug Alcohol Depend. 1995 Nov; 40:9–15.

***Give them constructive outlets to use their extra energy, such as sports, music, hobbies, and participation in weekend activities.*** The fact is that no one has sex 24/7, so the more we divert their attention and energy in productive directions, the less consuming sex becomes.

***Remind them that young women belong to someone and deserve respect.*** If a young woman is carrying herself in a disrespectful manner, that is an excellent reason to leave her alone but never a reason to disrespect her.

***Explain that the best way to prevent one thing from leading to another is to avoid doing that one thing in the first place.*** The best way to control a fire is to prevent it. Let's help our young men learn to avoid putting themselves in compromising situations.

Even with our best mentoring or parenting, our young men may still engage in premarital or unsafe sex. However, we can reduce the chances by interacting with them consistently and openly about the topic.

# Action Steps

*What efforts will you take to help young black men maintain a proper perspective toward the opposite sex?*

*How can you initiate candid conversations with young black men about the results of leading sexually active lives?*

# 6
# Handle. Your. Business.

*The problem isn't a lack of money; it's a lack of knowledge.*
*—Lee Jenkins*

Right now, you may be frustrated with your position in life and feel that you need to make some desperate changes in order to get ahead and live the life of your dreams. You may be financially astute and prosperous but feel discontent, knowing there must be more to life than acquiring money. To change our position, we must first change our disposition.

Remember, a change is not a change until *you* change. As a man, no matter how savvy, charming, or quick-witted you are, you must realize that everything has a process. Even after you set the plan for change in motion, the process will take time, and patience is required. A farmer doesn't sow a seed and come back the next day to see if it has sprouted. You must be willing to stay the course so you can reap the harvest.

Black men are powerful and eclectic beings. We are not all the same, and what is right for one is not necessarily right for another. However, one thing that we *all* deal with throughout our lifetime is money. So, with that said, let's explore the topic of how to build strong, economically productive black men.

## Mission Is More Than Money

Often I ask young men, "What are your future goals and dreams?" The answer is almost always centered on making a lot of money. As we further the discussion, I ask them how they plan to make money. Often their responses range from getting a job to getting a degree.

When I counsel young men about career options, I like to start with a personality test, such as the Myers-Briggs Type Indicator or the Kersey Temperament Sorter. It is important for me to help them figure out more about themselves and develop some insight into their strengths and weaknesses. Once a young man identifies, for example, that he is an introverted, contemplative type, we can explore career options that fit those traits.

I would rather help a young man discover high-paying careers that fit his passions and personality than just give him a list of the highest paying careers. If he has the interest and aptitude to be a brain surgeon or civil engineer, I want to help him to cultivate success in one of those fields. However, if he has the interest and aptitude to be a teacher or counselor, I can serve him just as well by helping him gain entrance into those careers as well.

Making money is not a problem. We are in favor of our young men making money and as much as their education, gifts, skills, talents, and ideas will allow. The trouble occurs when making money becomes the end result. I often hear avid sports fans saying things like "professional sports are all about money." I also hear these individuals asking, "What happened to playing for the love of the game?" When the mantra becomes "money at all costs," we lose meaning and we lose purpose. The love of the game succumbs to the love of the money.

As difficult as it may be for a boy to be patient and focus on his mission, it is important that we turn the focus there. We have seen two extremes. The first is a young man consumed by money and pursuing college degrees and seeking high-paying jobs while not understanding himself and his interests beyond just making money. The other extreme is a young man who does not have patience or a positive support system, so he seeks money by resorting to illegal activities such as selling drugs, robbery, and other criminal acts. In the former case, the young man is educated and is making money but finds himself empty and lost, because he found a career that paid him a lot of money but he did not find his mission. The latter ends up in the legal system, which minimizes his future choices and options. Contrary to what many think, money is not the root of all evil. The unhealthy love or greed for money within the heart of its possessor is what produces evil. Every day, we all have the option to choose to use our time, talent, and money for good or bad purposes.

In chapter 1, we discussed the fact that, in many cultures, boys participate in rites of passage as early as twelve years old. If a boy can assume manhood responsibilities as early as twelve, this suggests that black boys can become economically productive around this stage of life, if not earlier. While thinking with solutions in mind, we have to remind our young men of individuals like Farrah Gray, who became a millionaire at age fourteen. If he achieved millionaire status at fourteen, it is obvious that he was working on an idea or economically productive plan prior to that age. Gray in a CNN interview with Don Lemon quoted Mark Twain saying, "The two most important times... in anybody's life is when we were born and when we find out *why* we were born."

Gray discovered that he was an entrepreneur, a philanthropist, a motivational speaker, and an author. With proper guidance and mentoring, many more young black men can discover their mission and begin to operate in their purpose, living much more fulfilling lives as a result. However, as much as we would like for young black men to emulate Gray, the reality is that some young men seek a faster track to attaining money and fulfillment. With that thought in mind, let's dig a little deeper into the mindset of these young black men.

## My Mind on Your Money, And Your Money On My Mind

National juvenile crime statistics highlight that the most common crimes committed by juvenile boys are what we refer to as property crimes. These crimes involve taking someone else's property, whether it is their wallet, purse, or car. Often the purpose and result of these crimes is the acquisition of money; the property is sold for money or drugs. Money without mission makes money the end and the objective without regard to how it is obtained. If our young men lack the guidance and focus to make money legally by working a job or cultivating their talents and creating income, sometimes they resort to committing these property crimes with the purpose of acquiring money immediately. We should reinforce to our young men that it is wrong to steal the money and property of others. We should go deeper by discussing the work and time that it took for the individuals they have stolen from to attain their possessions. We must emphasize that obtaining monetary success is not as far from their reach as they may think. Acquiring material possessions is much more than a discussion of money; it is a discussion of a mentality and a thought process.

When I first started working in juvenile justice, I worked at a locked youth development center for juveniles who were convicted of felonies. We often sponsored special events such as guest speakers who we hoped could have a positive influence on our young men. The most indelible event occurred when we assembled a panel of distinguished business owners, court officials, and even a prosecutor. The business owners discussed the possibilities of making money legally through business ownership. They did a great job of highlighting both the work involved and the potential to make a lot of money. The court officials and the prosecutors encouraged our young men to seek entrepreneurial pursuits so that they could avoid being a part of the legal system.

At the end of the discussion, the panel took questions from the students. One of the first comments was a declaration that seemed to resonate with every young man in the room. The young man expressed his thoughts that the government puts drugs in black communities as a trap, and when black youth sell them, they get locked up. The prosecutor responded by saying something I will never forget: "If you know we are doing it, why do you keep taking the bait?" I have not stopped exploring that question: why do young black men in drug-infested areas keep taking the bait? In an effort to create solutions, I formed a drug dealer's treatment group for young men who had drug possession charges. Young men in that group told me that in their communities it was easier to sell drugs than to find a job. They also discussed the idea that selling drugs paid off quicker than waiting to get a job or a degree.

As I mentioned earlier, property crimes have a clear victim, as do violent crimes. As part of the program, our young men had to identify the victims of their crimes and describe how their crimes affected each victim. The exercise was a means for helping the students develop some measure of compassion for their victims.

> *Acquiring material possessions is much more than a discussion of money; it is a discussion of a mentality and a thought process.*

The students who had the most difficult time with this were the young men who were drug dealers. Many of the young men in my groups reported that selling drugs was better than robbing someone, because the "customers," as they are often called, willingly give up their money. Of course, an addict is not *willingly* doing anything, and I eventually address that issue in the treatment process. Before a student is deemed appropriate for treatment, he receives an assessment. The assessment questions help to gauge his level of compassion for others. When asked, "Is there anyone you would not have sold drugs to under any circumstance?" the majority of students answered, "My mother." or "One of my friend's mothers." Anyone else who had money or something else of value was a potential customer.

The "money by any means" mindset pushes morality to the side and unfortunately makes criminal behavior an option for some. What's the alternative? It is necessary to adopt a solutions-focused mindset, which will help these same industrious young men go from selling drugs to selling themselves.

## The Art of Selling Yourself

We have often heard it said that if you just do what you love, the money will come. We agree in part. One of the most productive discoveries is to discover oneself. It is to discover what drives you, what motivates you, and what you would do just for the love of it. Don't let anyone tell you that money does not matter. The message we most want young men to get is that money does matter, but it is not the most important matter. What matters most is that you are acquiring money legally and by doing something you love. The key is helping our young men learn to sell themselves. Selling has never been my strong suit. I tried to sell life insurance for two years. I worked hard, made phone calls, followed up on those phone calls, and at the end of the two years my net profit was around seven hundred dollars. I concluded that I was a horrible salesman.

When I started my private counseling practice, I gathered all of the consent forms, my professional disclosure statement, and other documentation and headed to my first in-home therapy appointment. I must have concealed my nervousness with enthusiasm because after the session the father of my client, who was in sales, exclaimed that I was a great salesman. I told him the story of my failed attempt at selling insurance and stated that I was surprised to hear him compliment my salesmanship. His reply was "You just sold *us* on your services!" The difference was that I had no real passion or interest in selling insurance, but I had a great deal of passion and interest in helping people through counseling. I had started selling insurance only to make money. When I started my practice, I found that people sought out my services. I did not have to make any calls; they called me. Focus on what you love, do it well, and the money will come.

## I Am Somebody

We often speak to young people about the importance of knowing their value and of seeing themselves as their greatest asset. You are defined by your character, your work ethic, and your ability to add value to the situations you find yourself in. Young black men should be encouraged to look at themselves the way Fortune 500 CEOs look at their corporations. When a CEO identifies unprofitable workers or strategies, they begin to trim the fat. In other words, in the business world, if it doesn't make money, it doesn't make sense, and it is ultimately dismissed.

*Black men must not passively wait for money to come to them, but rather be diligent in producing the type of work, products, and services that bring money to them and build wealth for generations.*

Our ability to work and provide for our families and ourselves is a hallmark of manhood, and whether we like it or not, men are viewed as providers and protectors. If young black men are not empowered to provide for themselves, how will they ever be able to lead and provide for a family? As a man, you were designed to be productive, creative, and resourceful. In order to build strong, economically productive black men, we must teach them that they are assets, not liabilities. They were created to add value and to be innovative.

Unfortunately, black history is often limited to the stories of a courageous, outspoken few. We must take the time to educate young black men about the incredible stories of men such as Lewis Latimer, the inventor of the light bulb's carbon filament, who worked alongside Thomas Edison and Alexander Graham Bell; Granville T. Woods, who left school at age ten to work and support his family and ultimately invented a train-to-train communication system; George Washington Carver, who, even though he didn't go to college until he was thirty, developed peanut butter and four hundred plant products; Garrett Morgan, who invented the gas mask and the first traffic signal light; and Lonnie G. Johnson, the inventor of the world-famous squirt water gun known as the Super Soaker.[19]

In the twenty-first century, Andre Young, known professionally as Dr. Dre, has made history by becoming the first black hip-hop artist/producer to achieve near-billionaire status due to his role in a partnership that led to the development of the Beats headphones line, which provides a more innovative way of listening to music—something he does every day as a veteran music producer and record executive. [20]

What are we trying to say? For hundreds of years, black men have been and remain innovative, productive, and responsible for many of the most important inventions known to mankind. There is no reason for us to let up now. Good ideas are worth nothing until a person or group of people successfully implements them. Companies are not profitable without diligent workers. Black men must not passively wait for money to come to them, but rather be diligent in producing the type of work, products, and services that bring money to them and build wealth for generations.

## Mission, Money, and Mental Health

The first mental health agency I worked for was one of the main service providers in our area. My first assignment was to work as a clinician on one of their largest grants. The organization secured the grant, which was for $144,000 per year and I worked on a team with two other therapists. Our combined salary with benefits came to around $90,000 per year. The remainder of the funds was designated for the company to use for any additional overhead expenses. The company embraced the risk of starting the organization; they did the work to secure the grant; and I agreed to the benefits package they offered. It was really none of my business as to what they did with the rest of the money. That is, it was none of my business until my supervisor included me in on the business without realizing it. Over the course of six months, both of my teammates resigned, and the company never hired anyone to replace them. Therefore my caseload tripled, but my pay remained the same. I did what I thought was right; I worked harder and developed a system for seeing the students on my caseload plus the additional students I inherited from the resignation of my teammates.

19 Scholastic Action Magazine, (Adapted February 21, 2000) http://teacher.scholastic.com/activities/bhistory/inventors/index.htm (June 15, 2013).
20 BBC News, Dr Dre: The first 'hip-hop billionaire', http://www.bbc.com/news/business-27350075 (Retrieved March 7, 2015).

During one of my scheduled supervisions, I walked into my supervisor's office, and he and the president of the company happened to be engaged in a conversation about me. When the president saw me, he shook my hand and thanked me for all of my hard work in the absence of the team members who resigned. He praised me for my diligence and efficiency. Then my supervisor said, "Let me show you how much money your work alone has drawn down for the company." I suppose he thought I would be even more proud of myself. However, the president interrupted and said, "No, don't show him that; he might ask for a raise!" I could not believe what was happening; I suppose he meant it as a joke, but I was not laughing. He assured me that the company would hire two others to replace the teammates. Once my supervision session started, the president exited the room, and my supervisor showed me the amount I had brought in. It was in excess of $50,000.

Eventually, the company did hire a part-time therapist, who resigned after only a few months, and one full-time therapist who worked with me for less than a year. It was not long before I would resign to accept another position. The lesson I learned was more valuable than a raise. I learned that my work was a great asset to the company and that I could take my gifts, talents, and work ethic and build my own business if I decided to do so.

Often I have seen young men seek affirmation of their value in the type of shoes they are able to purchase or the type of outfits they have hanging in their closets. There is nothing wrong with being well dressed. The concern arises when a young man believes his wardrobe or any other material possession gives him worth. It is paramount that young men are told—and that they believe—their true value lies within themselves.

We need to give our young men opportunities to understand that they possess the ability to create jobs and to make money for themselves. We should always promote the value of education while also teaching the value of entrepreneurship. The focus should rest on how we can help our young men believe that they possess the human capital required to create their own money.

## The Multiple Streams of Income Mindset

*Entrepreneurship is an option and should be explored by many young black men as a way to create the lifestyle of their dreams.*

As entrepreneurs who have experience on both sides of the corporate America fence, we highly recommend that young black men adopt a "multiple streams of income" approach toward employment and the achievement of financial solvency. There is no one-size-fits-all answer that we can supply, but for those desiring to do more than "just get by," we recommend adopting a proactive, entrepreneurial approach to making a living.

A black man's greatest wealth-building asset is his *ability to earn* income. Though not for everyone, entrepreneurship is an option and should be explored by many young black men as a way to create the lifestyle of their dreams. Many people do not make all the money they want to make from their main source of income. Encourage young black males to be innovative, resourceful, and productive. We recommend working toward the goal of having multiple streams of income to reduce numbers of poverty and unemployment. If managed properly, this additional income can be used to increase the net worth of the young black men of the next generation.

## Entrepreneurship

One of the realities that we choose not to shy away from is the fact that not everyone is cut out for corporate America. Some people prefer to work in an established, structured system and do very well for themselves in the process. However, another reality is that, in the twenty-first century and beyond, even recent college graduates who feel they do fit the corporate America mold are struggling to secure full-time employment. The days of telling youth to go to school to get a good education so that they can get a secure job are long gone. In fact, about half of recent college graduates might consider that advice to be archaic and even offensive.

College graduates face tremendous hurdles to becoming gainfully employed due to the overwhelming pool of both qualified and overqualified job applicants. According to a study by Rutgers University entitled *Chasing the American Dream: Recent College Graduates and the Great Recession*, only 51 percent of recent college graduates were employed full-time.[21] Our young black men are a part of this generation, and we must equip them for the realities that they face, not only after completing high school, but also after their postsecondary education. Even those college graduates who have secured full-time jobs are often disenchanted with their initial earnings in comparison to that of their counterparts who graduated years prior. In today's economy, it is very possible to work a full-time job and, after deducting taxes, medical insurance, and other benefits, not have enough income to make ends meet. Many are living paycheck to paycheck and often have *more month than money*. Since we cannot simply snap our fingers and create a more favorable economic outlook, we must focus on what we can change: our mindset. In his book *Cashflow Quadrant*, Robert Kiyosaki outlines the four different sectors that represent the means by which cash flows in our society: the employee, the self-employed, the business owner, and the investor. Employees work for others; self-

> *Working for yourself means making yourself work.*

---

21 Charley Stone, Carl Van Horn, & Cliff Zukav, Chasing the American Dream: Recent College Graduates and the Great Recession, (2012).

employed individuals work for themselves; business owners create a system and hire other people to work for them; and investors distribute capital to aspiring businesses and put their money to work in both the private and public sectors.

Today it is not uncommon to hear entrepreneurs talk about their business ideas and about living the dream. But please don't allow work-from-home advertisements that say working from home or working for yourself will be fast, easy money to deceive you. Working for yourself means making yourself work. Though you are working harder, you are doing the type of work you love, and have a greater vision for what you are working toward. So the real question is, are you ready to work like you never have in order to achieve success?

Here are some of the realities of entrepreneurship:

- You will have to work harder than you would if you were an employee.
- Expect *not* to make money at first. Most small businesses lose money in the early years.
- Being good at or even an expert in your craft or trade has nothing to do with successfully running a business. Being a great painter does not mean you will have the capacity to run a painting business.
- Expect to be misunderstood: being an entrepreneur means you will have to take risks, and many of your closest family and friends may not understand why you would want to take such chances.
- Entrepreneurship is not *only* about money, but also about a vision and a passion.

## A To-Do List for Entrepreneurs

- Spend time with other entrepreneurs and people who have vision.
- Spend less time with people who try to discourage your vision.
- Develop your skills because *you* are your greatest asset as an entrepreneur.
- Create a business plan and develop it as you learn.

We must undergo a major mental shift in order to experience business-related success. To be successful as entrepreneurs, we must no longer buy into the following:

- Our degrees and level of educational attainment will ensure that we make "good money."
- We will consistently receive a check once every week, every two weeks, or monthly because we were present and performed our work-related tasks.
- We can do the minimum amount of work required and our business will still prosper.
- Effective written and verbal communication is not that important.

- Our business will grow even if we don't invest any money in it.
- We can be successful without valuing people.
- Our good product or service will simply sell itself.

## Full-Time Employee/Part-Time Entrepreneur

To say the least, working for someone else and yourself at the same time is not easy. It requires a huge level of discipline and a willingness to delay gratification indefinitely and to be misunderstood often. You must be very sure of yourself, because you will have to refer frequently to your "why" as you pursue your dream. If you don't believe in your dream, no one else will. Many will question your priorities and try to send you on all-expense-paid guilt trips. It takes a strong, gutsy person to be an entrepreneur. You must not slack off on your current employer, even though you can see the proverbial light at the end of the tunnel. As you work for your current employer, remind yourself of the day that you interviewed for your job.

Are you sowing good seeds toward your employer daily? The seeds that you sow as an employee for others will be harvested in your future days as a business owner and employer of others. While working for others, model the mindset and practice the principles that you want your future employees to possess and practice. As the Golden Rule admonishes, "Do unto others as you would have them do unto you."

Based on the way you work and the value you bring to your current employer, would *you* hire you? Remember, there are only two positions in a job interview: the interviewer and the job seeker. Develop a plan of action and conduct yourself so that one day you will be the one *asking* the questions instead of the one answering them.

## Transitioning from Employee to CEO

The process of transitioning from one income source to another overwhelms many people. This is because we get comfortable with the familiar and resist change, even when it could be positive change. Here are some tips on transitioning from employee to business owner:

- Consider the natural gifts and talents you possess. How can you monetize these abilities?
- Assess your level of risk tolerance, then begin to take calculated risks.
- Embrace sacrifice; understand that the hours from 5:00 p.m. to 9:00 a.m. are just as important as the hours from 9:00 a.m. to 5:00 p.m. Establish and respect your business schedule like you do your work schedule.
- Invest in yourself. Spend money to make money.
- Don't quit.

## How Valuable Is Your Brand?

I recently asked a friend how much she thought the legendary fast-food chain McDonald's was worth. "Billions!" she instantly replied. "How do you know?" I asked. "The signs say *billions* served daily, plus the restaurants are always in prominent locations and are rarely empty." she replied.

I have to agree with her. Without question, McDonald's is an iconic brand. It's dependable, consistent, and convenient. You know exactly what to expect when you pull up to the drive-thru or walk up to the counter, yet they always seem to add something new to the menu to offer alternatives to their loyal customer base. McDonald's is probably telling the truth when they say "Billions served daily." What is even more powerful is that this phrase printed below the golden arches is confirmed over and over again, day after day, rain or shine.

What are you saying about yourself? What does your brand say about you? Would those who know you well use words like *dependable, consistent, innovative,* and *progressive* to describe your personal brand? One of the most important things a black man can do is continually seek to raise his value. Raising your value is not about increasing your net worth, but your self-worth. Like McDonald's, the more value you offer to others, the more valuable you are perceived to be by others. So how does a man raise his value? You will raise your value by consistently applying a well-established principle: the principle of giving.

## Giving As a Way of Living

It is truly better to give than to receive. Why? Because givers experience a boomerang effect when they release to the recipient. Based on the law of sowing and reaping, givers become receivers, and sowers become reapers. The law says, "You reap what you sow." Notice it doesn't say, "You reap *when* you sow." You reap *after* you sow. It also doesn't say *where* you will reap, but we'll talk about that a little later.

> *The more value you offer to the world, the more opportunity—and subsequently money—you position yourself to receive.*

When you smile at someone, you activate the power necessary to receive a smile in return. If you hold the door for someone, it's not uncommon for him or her to hold the next door for you. If you compliment waiters and waitresses on their service, you are likely to receive even better service. As the receiver, you experience only one side of the principle of giving. The buck stops with you until you activate your power to give.

On the other side of the equation, givers actually position themselves to receive infinitely because the release of their gift initiates a return, thus enabling them to give again and again. If you want to get a promotion on your job, it's obvious you won't get it by working with *less* passion and intensity. If you give the maximum effort possible, you position yourself to receive better results, which improve your employer's bottom line. The improvement of that bottom line usually means more money for the employer, and more money for them could mean a raise or promotion for you.

Does this always happen? No. We must warn you, as we mentioned earlier, that you may not always reap *where* you sow. A farmer knows that his harvest will develop in a specific geographic location: where he sows his crops. However, in the field of life, as seen earlier in Jeremiah's story about his entry into entrepreneurship, sometimes you may reap the benefits of your effort from another source or locale, such as a job offer from another employer with more pay or the launch of a new business. The key factor to remember is that *you*, the giver or planter, are the common denominator in all of these situations. The more value you offer to the world, the more opportunity—and subsequently money—you position yourself to receive.

As black men, we must look inside ourselves to assess our gifts, talents, strengths, and weaknesses. Knowing what you're *not* good at will help you to focus your efforts on building value and income in the area of your strengths. What gifts or talents do you have inside you that, when offered and released to the world, will create a great demand for you? What sacrifice might you need to make in order to build a strategy around how to release your gifts? You may need to isolate yourself in a quiet place away from the hustle, bustle, and noise so that you can think clearly and begin to put your plan together so that you can take action.

Whether you realize it or not, you might be a problem-solver, creator, author, inventor, builder, coach, motivator, teacher, or entrepreneur. The power to raise your value and change your position is in your hands. God has gifted each one of us with the innate ability to make our existing situation better. The circumstances of today don't have to be the fate of tomorrow. If we give more of ourselves to the process of becoming lifelong learners, we will reap the harvest of knowledge. Knowledge in and of itself has no power. Applied knowledge is what allows you to experience power.

Giving is not just a principle related to money. We are also able to give our time, talent, and encouragement. Black men must proactively seek ways to raise their public profile. We must frequently be caught doing good in our communities. As mentioned previously, the media often present lopsided images of black males participating in negative things such as criminal activity. As much as we may not like the inequities presented, the reality is that the teens and adult males on the screen are not dressed in "black face."

> *Knowledge in and of itself has no power. Applied knowledge is what allows you to experience power.*

Black males cannot afford, literally or figuratively, to be perceived as what I call *dormant doormats.* The word *dormant* means "a state of rest or inactivity." In addition to being a mat that people use to wipe their feet before entering a building, *doormat* is also defined as "a person who is the habitual object of abuse or humiliation by another." Those of us who are educated, gainfully employed, successful businessmen and committed husbands and fathers must reach back to our brothers and encourage them that they can do the same by offering a hand up, not a handout. We can reverse the rates of unemployment specific to black men, but to do so we must polish our soft skills and be as career-ready as the next candidate, regardless of race or gender.

## A Good Problem to Have

A man must first be able to provide for himself before he can provide for others. With all the career-related websites, publications, and resource centers in our communities, a young black man's greatest focus should be selecting the career path that is best for him; he should not be ignorant of the plentiful options that exist. Focusing on career development is very important. One practical approach is to conduct personality and talent assessments in order to direct them toward vocational paths that are both realistic and profitable, regardless of the chosen field. In an effort to help provide that direction, featured below are some of the fastest growing careers in the United States.

| OCCUPATION | MINIMUM REQUIRED EDUCATION | *MEDIAN PAY |
|---|---|---|
| **\*Heath Care** | | |
| Dental Hygienists | Associate's degree | $68,250 |
| Occupational Therapists | Master's degree | $72,320 |
| Physical Therapists | Doctoral or professional degree | $76,310 |
| Physician Assistants | Master's degree | $86,410 |
| Registered Nurse | Associate's degree | $64,690 |
| **\*Mental Health and Social Services** | | |
| Health Educators | Bachelor's degree | $45,830 |
| Counselors & Marriage & Family Therapists | Master's degree | $39,710 |
| Social Workers | Bachelor's or Masters degree | $42,480 |
| Substance Abuse & Behavioral Disorder Counselors | High school diploma or equivalent | $38,120 |

| OCCUPATION | MINIMUM REQUIRED EDUCATION | *MEDIAN PAY |
|---|---|---|

## *Education

| OCCUPATION | MINIMUM REQUIRED EDUCATION | *MEDIAN PAY |
|---|---|---|
| Elementary, Middle, and High School Teachers | Bachelor's Degree | $52,190 |
| Postsecondary Teachers | Doctoral or Professional Degree | $62,050 |
| Elementary, Middle, and High School Principals | Master's Degree | $86,970 |
| Postsecondary Education Administrators | Master's Degree | $83,710 |
| School and Career Counselors | Master's Degree | $53,380 |

## *Information Technology

| OCCUPATION | MINIMUM REQUIRED EDUCATION | *MEDIAN PAY |
|---|---|---|
| Computer Network Architects | Bachelor's degree | $45,830 |
| Information Security Analysts | Bachelor's degree | $45,830 |
| Network & Computer Systems Administrators | Bachelor's | $69,160 |
| Software Developers | Bachelor's degree | $90,530 |
| Web Developers | Bachelor's degree | $45,830 |

## *Arts And Design

| OCCUPATION | MINIMUM REQUIRED EDUCATION | *MEDIAN PAY |
|---|---|---|
| Multimedia Artists and Animators | Bachelor's Degree | $58,510 |
| Graphic Designers | Bachelor's Degree | $43,500 |
| Industrial Designers | Bachelor's Degree | $58,230 |
| Fashion Designers | High School Diploma | $64,530 |
| Art Directors | Bachelor's Degree | $80,630 |

| OCCUPATION | MINIMUM REQUIRED EDUCATION | *MEDIAN PAY |
|---|---|---|

## *Architecture and Engineering

| | | |
|---|---|---|
| Architects | Bachelor's Degree | $72,550 |
| Biomedical Engineers | Bachelor's Degree | $81,540 |
| Environmental Engineers | Bachelor's Degree | $78,740 |
| Surveyors | Bachelor's Degree | $54,880 |
| Petroleum Engineers | Bachelor's Degree | $114,080 |

## *Media and Communication

| | | |
|---|---|---|
| Audio and Video Equipment Technicians | Associates Degree or Vocational Certification | $39,870 |
| Producers and Directors | Bachelor's Degree | $68,440 |
| Public Relations Managers and Specialists | Bachelor's Degree | $57,550 |
| Interpreters and Translators | Bachelor's Degree | $43,300 |

## Installation, Maintenance, and Repair

| | | |
|---|---|---|
| Automotive Body and Glass Repairers | High School Diploma | $37,580 |
| Automotive Service Technicians and Mechanics | High School Diploma | $35,790 |
| Medical Equipment Repairers | Associates Degree | $44,490 |
| Heating, Air Conditioning, and Refrigeration Mechanics and Installers | High School Diploma, Vocational Certification, Some states require a license | $42,530 |
| Diesel Service Technicians and Mechanics | High School Diploma, Vocational Certification | $40,850 |

| OCCUPATION | MINIMUM REQUIRED EDUCATION | *MEDIAN PAY |
|---|---|---|
| **\*Transportation and Material Moving** | | |
| *Heavy and Tractor-Trailer Truck Drivers* | *High School Diploma, Commercial Driver's License* | *$37,770* |
| *Airline and Commercial Pilots* | *Complete civilian flight school, Commercial Pilot's License* | *$92,060* |
| *Subway and Streetcar Operators* | *High School Diploma, On-the-job Training* | *$56,880* |
| *Water Transportation Occupations* | *Transportation Worker Identification Credential (TWIC), Merchant Marine Credential (MMC)* | *$46,610* |

22

[22] Bureau Of Labor Statistics; Occupational Outlook Handbook; http://www.bls.gov/ooh/home.htm (Retrieved September 16, 2014).

# Action Steps

*How can you instill the value of developing a personal mission in the young men you influence?*

*In what specific ways can you help to build strong, economically productive black men?*

# PART III

**Brilliant Or Broken?**

**Don't Get Mad... Get Busy!**

# 7
# Brilliant Or Broken?

*You can give people money, but you can't make them stay rich. You can't take away an education—it's an intellectual property that will keep you rich forever.*
—Dr. Steve Perry

Do black boys really have learning challenges? Are black boys lazy? Or, are they simply misguided and misdiagnosed? The brilliance of black boys can be overshadowed by emotional, behavioral, and mental health problems. So are black male students brilliant or broken?

> *Sometimes the odds really are stacked against you, but that does not mean you have to fail.*

In the first grade, I was labeled with a learning disability. My mother was notified that I would need remedial help, and I was placed in the lowest reading group. I was able to read, but was timid and scared to speak up. I said nothing when asked to read. To make matters worse, I had a speech impediment, which made it very difficult to understand anything I said. I was a classic at-risk child; who had trouble speaking clearly, was labeled as learning disabled, was being raised by a single mother, and lived in a low-income housing project. On paper, they might as well have reserved a prison cell for me, because with my specific set of problems, what else could anyone expect of me? Sometimes the odds really are stacked against you, but that does not mean you have to fail. My mother refused to buy into the limitations that were placed on me by the school. She insisted that I do extra reading at home; I read with my uncle, with her, and to myself when no one else was available. She also accepted the help offered by the school, including speech therapy and other academic assistance programs. My issue was not one of ability but of confidence. Once my confidence grew, my teachers began to see that I was as capable as any other student.

For students who have specific learning challenges, the Individualized Education Program (IEP) exists to provide educational assistance and support to enhance the opportunity for success in the academic setting.[23] In addition to school-based programs, afterschool initiatives and a host of tutoring and mentoring programs are available in school districts across the country. The resources are growing for students in special education, and I have personally worked with many programs designed to assist students who have special needs. Given the available resources, why do our young men continue to lead in school suspensions, dropouts, and juvenile adjudications? My experience has shown that often our young men don't lack the ability or the resources to achieve academically—they lack the will. There are two key factors that kill their will.

**Being judged by a label.** When children are labeled as having borderline mental functioning or being marginally or mildly retarded, how do you think they feel about themselves? Once a child garners a label, it is difficult for him to break through the stigma attached to it. Labels set a proverbial glass ceiling and often drive the direction that a child's life takes. Before I review a medical record or file, I make it a point to meet my client in person. I do not want his label to influence how I interact with him. I have engaged in numerous discussions with other professionals who have been surprised when a child performs above and beyond his mental health diagnosis. It does not take long before young men with such labels give up and perform down to who they think they are. Labels exact a toll on the self-esteem, especially when their peers are privy to their special-needs label. Slowly the school and academic settings become a traumatizing experience, and it is not long before they devise schemes to get out of that environment.

**Misdiagnosis of mental health disorders.** Mental health disorders are real, and they do impair people in a variety of ways. However, clinicians should use care and precision when making a diagnosis. Due to the managed-care system and the need to diagnose a disorder to receive payment, clinicians are often under pressure to diagnose symptoms quickly. Often they arrive at a diagnosis after only a brief interaction with a child. The clinician needs to conduct a comprehensive clinical evaluation to rule out other conditions that mirror certain disorders. If a disorder exists, I am an advocate for treatment by all means. I am not even opposed to the

---

23 Office of Special Education and Rehabilitative Services U.S. Department of Education, *A Guide to the Individualized Education Program* (Maryland: Editorial Publications Center U.S. Department of Education, 2000).

use of medication as long as a physician manages it closely and the child receives simultaneous therapeutic and skill-building resources. Depending on the severity of the disorder, medication may be needed to help manage the symptoms while the child is participating in therapy.

> *We must remember to teach viable coping and social skills that will serve them far better and far longer than the medication.*

The emphasis should be placed on therapy and the acquisition of academic, social, and coping skills. The medication helps the child focus long enough to learn the skills being taught. If medication is used as a panacea in exclusion of therapeutic interventions and skills development, the child is not equipped or empowered to cope with his mental health problems. In effect, the disorder may be a convenient crutch for him to use when he simply wants to avoid exerting his full effort.

Many of the young men I have worked with therapeutically have accepted the idea that they are not capable of exerting mental effort or exercising restraint unless they are on their medication. I am weary of hearing jokes such as "Billy was acting out in class today. I can tell somebody forgot to give him his medication." However, we must remember to teach viable coping and social skills that will serve them far better and far longer than the medication.

So, what do we do if a child in the academic setting has an accurately diagnosed disorder? I suggest therapy that focuses on the following components:

- *Behavior therapy.* Teaches the family ways to help manage the child's behavior. They may learn behavior modification techniques and ways to build the parent/child relationship.
- *Talk therapy.* Helps to build a child's self-esteem. The child has an outlet to express his thoughts and feelings. He may also learn alternative ways to deal with day-to-day challenges and concerns. The therapist can help him learn to cope with his symptoms in a proactive way.
- *Social skills training.* Teaches the child better skills for playing and interacting with other children. The therapist may practice and model common social skills for the child, such as listening to others, sharing, waiting one's turn, or appropriately interrupting the teacher. The child may also practice interpersonal communication skills like perceiving both verbal and nonverbal cues, such as facial expressions and tone of voice.
- *Parent training.* Parents may also learn ways to structure situations to help allow their children to succeed. For example, allowing only one playmate at a time might help the child remain calm. If a child has trouble completing tasks, parents may learn to help the child divide a large task into smaller steps and praise the child after each step is completed.
- *Family support groups.* Allows groups of parents to share their experiences and concerns. Support groups may also share information and referrals to specialists, and invite experts to speak.

When a child is accurately diagnosed and provided with treatment that empowers him, his family, and other caregivers, he has a great chance of developing adaptive coping skills that will serve as an asset as he continues to grow and develop. He can also learn to cope with his challenges in the school setting rather than giving up or depending on medication, which only provides temporary relief.

## The Act-Out-to-Get-Out Cycle

My private practice caseload was full of young men who had encountered frustration and failure in the educational setting. Many of my clients were on medication and had spent time suspended or expelled from school. When they did attend school, many of them were described as zombie-like because of the menu of medications they were taking. When a child is acting out and is in the midst of a group of other children, the tendency is to remove the child from the group. This tendency may take the form of a time-out, in-school suspension, out-of-school suspension or expulsion. Once he is placed out of the school setting, we have isolated him from his potential support network. I do understand the reasons behind removing a child who is being disruptive. "Discipline" that isolates saves the environment from the child, but who saves the child?

> *"Discipline" that isolates saves the environment from the child, but who saves the child?*

The core purpose of discipline is to teach a child appropriate behaviors. Often the suspended or expelled student is left to his own devices, and his isolation may become a breeding ground for anger or embarrassment, which may grow into resentment and despondency. Once he loses hope, he is an easy target for delinquency, and then we have to deal with his needs in the juvenile or adult correctional system. To prevent young men from taking this path of hopelessness, let's look at some specific strategies to help keep them in class when they act out.

- Provide them with opportunities to receive positive attention.
- Draw attention to their positive attributes.
- Remember the proverb "It takes a village to raise a child." It also takes a village to educate a child. Identify teachers, coaches, custodians, or school volunteers that can help provide positive reinforcement.
- Use role-plays and interactive activities in the classroom when appropriate.
- If available, utilize media and technology to make the classroom a dynamic and attractive place in which students will want to stay and participate.
- If he has an Individualized Education Program (IEP), review the details of the program to make sure he is getting his specific needs met.
- If he does not have an IEP, he may need to begin the process.

I understand that teaching and counseling are different disciplines: teachers have the job of instructing, and counseling is more process-oriented. Teachers simply don't have time to process the often complicated reasons for acting-out behavior. However, when students are sent out for acting out, they are neither receiving instruction nor processing their problems. It is not uncommon for a student to just sit in the hallway, in school suspension, or in the principal's office in silence with the work they were either not able or willing to do in the first place. Often a young man acts out to get out for a reason. Our job as professionals is to find out *why* and to work to surround him with relevant resources. He may not feel confident in the academic environment because of past failures or negative experiences, or he may be having a family or personal problem. If he is just sent out, we miss an opportunity to meet his needs with school or community-based resources.

*If we allow our young men to continue to achieve absurdly low goals in the academic setting, they will be ill-prepared to function in a society that will demand more.*

Over the following pages we will explore some additional strategies to help build a young man's will to stay engaged in the academic environment:

***Help him make a connection to art, music, or athletics.*** These activities allow him the chance to connect to his gifts and talents that may not have room to shine in the academic environment. Harvard education professor Dr. Howard Gardner developed the Theory of Multiple Intelligences that highlights areas of intelligence human beings possess in varying degrees. The seven intelligences he detailed in his book *Frames of Mind* are visual-spatial, bodily kinesthetic, musical, interpersonal, intrapersonal, linguistic, and logical-mathematical.[24] Gardner's work is a product of extensive research, and despite its critics, it offers viable options for children who may not excel in the traditional academic settings. Traditional academic environments are often structured around linguistic and logical-mathematical proficiencies, but a child may be more gifted in spatial, interpersonal, or kinesthetic intelligence. A child may not excel in mathematics, but he may be gifted and competent in his ability to relate to and understand others, or his bodily-kinesthetic ability to participate in martial arts, dance, or athletics. The chart below shows how different types of children function and what they need.

24 Howard Gardner, *Frames of Mind: The Theory of Multiple Intelligences* (New York: Basic Books, 2004).

| Children who are strongly: | Think ... | Love ... | Need ... |
|---|---|---|---|
| *Linguistic* | *in words* | *reading, writing, telling stories, playing word games, etc.* | *books, tapes, writing tools, paper, diaries, dialogues, discussion, debate, stories* |
| *Logical-Mathematical* | *by reasoning* | *experimenting, questioning, figuring out puzzles, calculating, etc.* | *things to explore and think about, science materials, manipulatives, trips to the planetarium and science museum* |
| *Spatial* | *in images and pictures* | *designing, drawing, visualizing, doodling, etc.* | *art, LEGOs, videos, movies, slides, imagination games, puzzles, illustrated books, trips to art museums* |
| *Bodily-Kinesthetic* | *through somatic sensations* | *dancing, running, jumping, building, touching, gesturing, etc.* | *role-play, drama, movement, things to build, sports and physical games, tactile experiences, hands-on learning* |
| *Musical* | *via rhythms and melodies* | *singing, whistling, humming, tapping feet and hands, listening, etc.* | *sing-along time, trips to concerts, music playing at home and school, musical instruments* |
| *Interpersonal* | *by bouncing ideas off other people* | *leading, organizing, relating, manipulating, mediating, partying, etc.* | *friends, group games, social gatherings, community events, clubs, mentors/apprenticeships* |
| *Intrapersonal* | *deeply inside themselves* | *setting goals, meditating, dreaming,* | *secret places, time alone, self-paced projects, choices* |

***Consistent physical exercise.*** Research in exercise physiology continues to confirm that exercise enhances energy and even helps improve mental health conditions such as depression and ADHD. In his book *Spark,* John Ratey, MD, highlights studies that show how elevating the heart rate to a certain level during aerobic exercise helps students make dramatic academic improvements.[25] Given the importance of exercise as well as the lack of exercise among children, we have movements in our country that focus on the importance of just getting up and moving for at least an hour a day. With video games, Internet, and media entertainment all around us, something as fundamental as exercise can succumb to the lure of the couch and the entertainment system of choice.

---

25 John Ratey, *Spark: The Revolutionary New Science of Exercise and the Brain* (New York, Little, Brown and Company, 2008).

*Set attainable goals, but set them high.* It is important for young men with learning challenges to achieve goals as a means of building their confidence and esteem. If we allow our young men to continue to achieve absurdly low goals in the academic setting, they will be ill-prepared to function in a society that will demand more. Young men lose the motivation to work when they do not have to exert much effort to achieve the goals set for them. Let's set attainable goals but set them high enough that young men have to exert effort. They may not reach all the goals, but they will have stretched and challenged themselves, which is a part of their growth and development.

*Emphasize building life skills.* A young man with a mental health disorder is best served by the acquisition of skills. If he has a problem with anger or attention, skills such as communication, conflict resolution, and organization will serve him well. We have to do more than just tell him he can do better. We have to show him specifically how and give him room to practice and develop those skills so that he can grow to be self-reliant.

*Connection with a role model and mentor.* Young men need tangible examples by which to model their behavior. It helps them to talk with someone who has overcome similar challenges and who can guide them through some of the specific steps needed to gain success in school and other endeavors. Often young men lose their will if they believe it is impossible to overcome their challenges, but having mentors gives them real models for success. Often they feel comfortable addressing questions and concerns with their mentor that they are reluctant to discuss with a teacher or administrator.

## Does Having a Black Male Teacher Matter?

It is no secret that black males are severely underrepresented in the teaching profession. It is highly likely in America, even in urban or inner-city school districts, that a black child could go through his entire K–12 education experience without having one black man as a teacher. Less than 2 percent of America's teachers are black men.[26] Is this a cause for concern? It is certainly worth discussing as it relates to how we educate young black men. Arne Duncan, the current US Secretary of Education, launched the Teach Campaign in an effort to recruit more African American men to enter the teaching profession straight out of college.

As an educator, I can say that it did make a difference in the lives of the black male students in my classes—particularly those from single-parent, mother-led homes—to see me as an educational authority figure. Since many of our boys have

---

26 Ivory A. Toldson, Black Male Teachers: Becoming Extinct? http://www.theroot.com/articles/culture/2013/04/black_male_teacher_shortage_debunking_the_ myth.3.html (Retrieved June 15, 2013).

white females as their educator, the black vs. white cultural barrier can easily come into play. What does this do to the psyche of our children as it relates to their educational experience? For one, it significantly reduces the number of black boys that respond to questions about their career aspirations with the word *teacher*. Seeing primarily white, female teachers throughout your K–12 experience communicates that being a schoolteacher is not a viable career option for a black man.

> *The right teacher with the right understanding of the plight black males face in the education system can be a powerful motivator toward the pursuit of a college education in the future.*

Teachers spend as much time Monday through Friday with a child as his parent or guardian does. Simply stated, the teacher, not the parent, is positioned to be the educational authority in the life of a child. Parents should certainly be the first and ultimately, the most tenured teachers and champions of education in the lives of their children. Teachers have an extraordinary opportunity to shape the educational experiences of young black men in the formative years of their lives. The right teacher with the right understanding of the plight black males face in the education system can be a powerful motivator toward the pursuit of a college education in the future. There are countless people—from the rich and famous to local, unsung heroes—that pay homage to former teachers as the catalysts to their personal career trajectory.

## Too Cool for School

We should not expect the school system to be the only educator of our children; parents, extended family members, and the community play a key role in the education process. I have been in repeated situations where parents have brought their sons to me desperate for assistance. Their sons were having trouble in school, and they blamed the teachers and the educational system for it. They asked me to speak with the teachers about their sons' needs. Yet many teachers say the parents are the ones to blame for young men's struggles in the classroom. Why is it so important to determine whose fault it is? Let's imagine for a moment that we are able to identify the true culprit. Then what? Determining who is responsible for a young man's poor performance in school is futile unless we are working equally as hard to solve his educational problems.

It will take the parents, grandparents, aunts, uncles, and guardians pulling together with teachers and administrators to help our young men. Our collective focus has to remain on keeping them in school. If school does not provide a source of validation for a child, he will gravitate toward people and places that offer the support he craves. In the best-case scenario, he is validated through sports or some other extracurricular activity. In the worst case, he finds it in his relationships with negative peers. I have seen this pattern far too often.

Once a young black man begins to get suspended from school, he loses a major pro social influence in his life. The school may not need or want him, but he needs school. Keeping him in school ensures that he will not be left unsupervised in the community. It is perplexing when a child is suspended from school for skipping school. What he wants is to be out of school, so suspending him gives him what he wants but not what he needs. What can we do to address the problem? Here are two specific ideas that can help keep our young men in school:

- *Open communication between parents and teachers.* It is crucial that parents and teachers communicate openly together and offer each other mutual support . As difficult as it may be at times, both parties have to resist the urge to attack and blame the other. It is important that parents and teachers see themselves on the same team for the greater good of the child. I often hear parents and teachers talking *about* each other, but they have to talk *to* each other. Often teachers and parents don't talk until both are frustrated and tired. Frequent communication is ideal, and it is best at neutral times before there has been an escalation or a specific problem to address.

- *Identify legitimate learning disabilities and/or mental health disorders early.* If we can identify problems in the early elementary years, it is much easier to correct rather than waiting until the young man is a teen. Again, a careful evaluation of a child's mental state is important, because we do not want him misdiagnosed and because early treatment is very helpful. Working together may mean specialized plans (IEPs), bringing in specialists, and offering therapy. However, it is much more productive to do this sooner than later.

## Unclogging the Pipeline

Frederick Douglass once said, "It is easier to build strong children than to repair broken men." The "cradle to prison pipeline" is the moniker given to the national crisis occurring at the intersection of poverty and race that puts black boys at a one-in-three lifetime risk of going to jail.[27] If we truly want to see an increase in the number of black males enrolling in and completing college, we must start exercising our initiative much earlier than the high school years. We must start in the early, formative years.

By the time a young man has reached high school, he has already developed a mindset about education and about his role as a participant in the education process. This K-12 experience, whether good or bad, will have an undeniable

---

27 The Children's Defense Fund, http://www.childrensdefense.org/child-research-data-publications/data/cradle-prison-pipeline-report-2007-full-highres.html#updates (Retrieved October 5, 2013).

influence on his post–high school plans. For example, many young black boys have been retained repeatedly in the education system year after year, or even worse, have been "passed on" due to having been labeled discipline problems. Perceived as being perpetually incapable of performing at grade level, they can easily develop a disdain for education. Add to that the fact that they have been made to feel unwelcome by administrators and teachers via the constant receipt of both in and out-of-school suspensions, and you've got a major dilemma. These marks won't simply disappear with an eleventh-hour waving of the magical college access wand!

We must begin to acknowledge our responsibility to begin cultivating the academic potential of young black boys early during the elementary years. Succeeding in the academic environment has a lot to do with the parental and community focus on developing and strengthening the soft skills of our young black men. What are soft skills? They are the qualities, habits, attitudes, and abilities that allow us to function interpersonally in everyday life. The presence or absence of these skills can make or break our young black men academically.[28]

As an educator, I recommend that the village of parents, guardians, grandparents, mentors, and churches make a special ongoing effort to develop young black boys and teenagers in the soft skills areas listed below.

***Work ethic.*** This is established early by assigning and teaching them to complete tasks, chores, and responsibilities around the home, such as taking out the garbage, washing dishes and laundry, mowing the lawn, and checking the mailbox.

*Classroom connection:* When a teacher or adult in the academic environment gives instructions or assignments, students respond positively as they are accustomed to receiving and completing responsibilities in their home environment.

***Communication skills.*** Engage in frequent conversations with young black men by talking with them, not *at* them. Leave discussions about the weather to meteorologists! Talk with them about socially relevant issues using appropriate vocabulary and a reassuring tone of voice. Explain the difference between an indoor and an outdoor voice. Inform them that they do not address adults and authority figures as they would their friends. Model *how to listen* attentively and to avoid interrupting by patiently awaiting their turn to speak or reply.

*Classroom connection:* This reduces school-related infractions related to excessive or inappropriate communication. They will be empowered for self-advocacy and equipped to interact successfully with teachers, adults, and peers.

---

28 Kate Lorenz, http://jobs.aol.com/articles/2009/01/26/top-10-soft-skills-for-job-hunters/ (Retrieved October 7, 2013).

*Problem-solving skills.* Many students struggle in mathematics because of its formulaic processes. Omit one key fact or figure, and the entire equation will be incorrect. Help them practice by writing out hypothetical word problems using numerals or online tutorial resources involving addition, subtraction, multiplication, and division.

*Classroom connection: This reduces intimidation and confusion experienced in class and end-of-grade testing situations. It also makes it easier to identify important facts, figures, and successfully recognize the language that guides them to the correct problem-solving approach.*

*Working in groups or teams.* Explain that working with others is often not optional but a requirement, both in school and in work settings. Talk about the importance of respecting the opinions of others, while confidently sharing their point of view. Encourage them to be contributors. As an educator, I have seen far too many young black males attempt to hide or disappear in group settings instead of taking leadership roles.

*Classroom connection: Often, when teachers assign group work, the group members all receive the same grade. These are special opportunities for young black males to experience leadership and to develop impromptu interpersonal communication skills by being visible and "present" in the group setting.*

*Self-confidence.* In chapter 1, we discussed that knowing one's identity is pertinent to becoming a strong black man. A young man's confidence is, in many ways, connected to his self-worth. If he perceives himself as valuable, he will carry himself and interact with others according to that value. Self-confidence in public is a by-product of being validated in private.

*Classroom connection: Confident students are visible to teachers. They make healthy contributions to the classroom environment. They may find themselves frequently selected for in-class leadership roles and recommended for extracurricular student development opportunities such as camps and debate teams.*

## The Greatest Risk of All

As someone who counsels young men who have been incarcerated and have extreme behavior problems, it is always good to remind myself that the majority of young black males are not emotionally, mentally, or behaviorally disturbed. Despite troubling statistics and common perception, the majority of America's black males will never make their residence a state facility. They will not commit a violent crime, traffic drugs, join a gang, or participate in a drive-by shooting.[29] Yes, gang violence, the drug culture, and incarceration have devastated our young men, but high-risk behaviors are far less troubling than the risk of mediocrity.

Two of the greatest risks facing our young men are the lack of motivation and discipline to finish a task, and being content with just receiving a passing grade. We are at risk of being content living below our potential and doing just enough. It is easy to settle into the lull of being better than the guys who do participate in extreme negative behaviors. If someone challenges a young man's lack of drive, he can always say something like "At least I am not in prison or selling drugs." We have set the bar low for our young men. Staying out of prison and not trafficking drugs have become accomplishments. However, our young men are capable of much more. Finishing high school with a diploma is an important accomplishment, but it can't end there. The diploma is a key piece of a puzzle that extends beyond high school. College or vocational education is an important next step in the journey.

> *Yes, gang violence, the drug culture, and incarceration have devastated our young men, but high-risk behaviors are far less troubling than the risk of mediocrity.*

Being content to underachieve and do just enough to avoid incarceration is not enough. For example, a young man who is well behaved, a C student, has a part-time job, and respects his parents and other elders may not appear on the radar as an at-risk youth. Sure, he is not at immediate risk of the severe and extreme behaviors and the consequence mentioned earlier, but he is at risk. The fact that he is good could very well lull him into complacency. If his aim is to be able to say that he is "not that bad," he may never be as great as he could be. Here are some ways to help young men avoid mediocrity:

- *Encourage them to discover their passions and natural gifts as a complement to their academic responsibilities.* If their interests, such as music or mechanics, can be identified and cultivated, they may be able to move into that area and enjoy a fulfilling life that allows them to offer their gifts to the world.
- *Explain that school is preparation for the rest of their lives.* The secondary school experience is only thirteen years long, but serves as a foundation for them to build on for the rest of their lives. It is best for them to learn as much as possible, as opposed to just seeing school as an obstacle course to clear so they can enjoy the rest of their lives. Education is a key to helping make the rest of their lives productive and enjoyable.
- *Expose them to at least one marketable skill or trade.* We live in a technologically advanced culture. However, until our smartphones are

---

29 U.S. Department of Justice, http://ojjdp.gov/pubs/244476.pdf (Retrieved November 17, 2013).

smart enough to unstop sinks, lay brick, hammer nails, rotate tires, and wire light fixtures, we will need skilled labor. Learning to use our hands skillfully provides an additional means of income and a source of self-esteem and productivity. As we discussed in chapter 1, it can also serve as a platform for bonding and other life lessons.

- *Emphasize the importance of lifelong learning.* It is important that we help our young men stop asking questions such as: "Will this be on the test?" and "Is this for a grade?" If they are just trying to pass a school test, they may not be ready for the real tests that will come in life. Let's help our young men focus on how passing a test is only part of the test. The real value comes from the process of studying for and passing tests. Preparation for school tests teaches us how to study, manage time, and prepare. Those skills will serve them well beyond the grading period. It is important that we point out that learning begins at graduation.

## College Is a Good Choice for Many, But Not for All

The majority of young people who go to college do so initially because someone told them to. "Go to college so that you can graduate and get a good job" is the admonition that people were giving their children thirty years ago. This advice was given by a generation of people that did not have the smorgasbord of options and opportunities currently available to youth in the twenty-first century. What was once considered to be the formula for securing a stable job and secure lifestyle is no longer the sole recipe for success. This is questionable due to the surge of people that are completing bachelor's degree programs online resulting in a job market saturated with unemployed, college-degree wielding candidates. Do most people actually take the time to ponder the value of a college education? The truth is that going to college does not guarantee career success. It is true that your earning power increases when you obtain a postsecondary degree, but long-term financial success has more to do with the choices and decisions we make after college, how we manage and invest the money we earn, and the drive we possess.

College access initiatives—programs designed to increase opportunities to enter post-secondary education—are plentiful across the United States. We are living in arguably the most educated generation of this country's history.[30] In theory, encouraging young people to go to college and get a degree is sound advice and ends up being beneficial for most who graduate. Many black male students take the advice to apply and eventually enroll in college, but, with all the effort spent on getting them to apply and enroll in college, why are so many black males failing to graduate? What happens after these young men arrive on campus? What are the often-overlooked barriers to college completion? In order

---

30 U.S. Department of Education, http://nces.ed.gov/pubs2014/2014083.pdf (Retrieved November 29, 2013).

to reach President Obama's vision to double the college graduation rate by 2020, there must be solutions to the problems that cause this low college completion rate. Let's explore some of the barriers to college access and completion for black males.

*Poor planning.* If there's anything that hinders our black men's ability to attend college it's poor planning. Planning for college is an active process with clear steps and measurable deadlines. These steps should actually be put in writing in middle school. You may ask, "Why middle school? Isn't that too early to be focused on college?" No, it is not too early. Upon completion of the middle school years, students are facing their last four years of secondary school, so having a postsecondary education plan is important. To increase the college enrollment numbers of black men, there must be significant exposure to the college experience (campus visits and academic courses) and career-based curriculum starting in middle school. As a former AVID (Advancement Via Individual Determination) coordinator, one of my most impactful tasks was guiding students through a six-year plan featured in the college and career curriculum. Simple but effective, this plan was actually initiated with students in sixth grade, and if done correctly, would keep them on track over the next six years to enter a college or postsecondary institution upon high school graduation.

What if your school district is not fortunate enough to have college preparatory curriculum? Create your own plan. Start immediately wherever they are, regardless of age or grade level. By making a written plan a priority, we help young black men to know what they often *don't* know: how to get from wherever they are to the college campus. You can run toward a vision only when it is clear and in writing. Remember that a written plan is valuable only if you implement the steps that were written. All the planning in the world won't help you if you don't identify and meet mandatory application deadlines for admission, financial aid, scholarships, course registration, and tuition.

Confirm with your local school district and high schools that they offer courses that correspond to the admission requirements of the flagship public university of your state. Get to know the guidance counselors and academic advisers personally at your son's, nephew's, grandson's, or mentee's high school. These are the people that can help you. They should be accountable and responsible enough to answer any questions you have regarding what classes to take each year at the high school level in order to meet the freshman eligibility standards at the college of their choice. Remember, failing to plan is planning to fail.

*Academically unprepared.* If poor planning is number one, poor academic preparation is a close second when considering the barriers to college that young black men face. Many things compete for the attention of young men: girls, sports, television, the Internet, etc. There are simply too many of our young black men being passed along through the system because of "discipline problems." Some kids act out, not because they're uninterested in learning, but because they are bored. Reputations for disruptive behavior precede many of our boys, so new teachers label them before attendance is taken on the first day of school. If these boys sense that there is no expectation for them to perform academically, they will live up to that expectation. This is true for both the classroom and away from the classroom. If a young man is disengaged in the classroom, how in the world do you suppose he will engage in homework and studying away from school? It won't happen, because he didn't learn the basics in class that would allow him to help himself.

> *The school cannot be the only place where our young black men have conversations about academics.*

The fact remains that not all students learn the same. Different students perform at different levels in different learning environments. We can't allow them to struggle academically through elementary and middle school and expect them to simply "quit tripping" and "kick it into high gear" as juniors or seniors in high school. It's too late! As fathers, mentors, and vested stakeholders, we must talk to our young men early about not only the importance of studying, but *how* to study. Most students, even those in college, don't know how to study or take good notes. They must learn how to identify the *who, what, when, where, and how* of a lesson, whether it is delivered online or via lecture in a classroom.

As an educator, I am very familiar with what goes on in a classroom, and it takes an exceptional amount of patience and fortitude to do what a teacher does every day. Teachers attempt to manage a classroom of multiple personalities from diverse backgrounds and teach a subject at the same time. Unfortunately, most of the time, teachers don't actually get to *teach* for an entire class period. They also don't have extra class time to repeat the content over and over again at the middle and high school levels. Instead of blaming them, we must remember that teachers are only required to teach. It takes a special person to care. It's not the teacher's sole responsibility to ensure a student succeeds academically. That is also the role of the student's support network. The school cannot be the only place where our young black men have conversations about academics. We must make the time to find out where they are struggling academically and seek out academic assistance, if necessary. There are often free resources available, such as tutoring provided by the school district, that are not taken advantage of by our young men. Many schools and teachers offer tutoring before school hours or after school. Academic success is not accidental. Sometimes poor academic performance is simply the result of poor habits and the ineffective behaviors that we allow. Academic success is much more likely if we teach and model the development of good scholastic habits early in life.

**First-generation students.** Another myth is that if a young man has at least one parent or guardian in the home that has a college degree, he will master the college admissions and enrollment process. The truth is that some of those homes don't produce college-bound black males. How does this happen? People are busy and don't make the time to ensure that their children are adequately prepared for postsecondary education. They may assume that guidance counselors at their high school are doing all the heavy lifting in terms of college planning, exposure, and admissions. We must stop presuming and become extra careful to ensure that black males are receiving plentiful access to the college readiness information and programming available to them.

In the black community, we need to note some specific challenges. First, having no immediate family members that can speak from their personal college experience is a huge hurdle. Being the first in your family to attend college can be a challenge regardless of ethnicity. If our young men have limited exposure to black people, particularly black males, with college degrees, they might think that college just isn't for them. Also, not wanting to be labeled the "college boy" or appearing to be more fortunate than others is a tension felt by many a would-be college-bound black male student. Yes, the infamous "crabs in a bucket" mentality adversely affects both the younger and the older members of the black race.

In previous generations, it was possible to secure a long-term career without a college education. By 2020, 65 percent of all jobs will require postsecondary education and training. Of those jobs, 35 percent will require at least a bachelor's degree.[31] This means it is no longer an option but a necessity for black males, first-generation or not, to be abundantly represented on college campuses and completing degree programs in postsecondary education.

***Lack of money.*** This is self-explanatory. College is not free. If you don't believe you can afford it, your motivation and enthusiasm for attending college will be easily curbed. As a culture, we must talk more about the importance of 529 plans in our homes and social circles. A 529 plan is a tax-advantaged savings plan sponsored by a state, state agency, or educational institution designed to encourage saving for future college costs. The plan is authorized by section 529 of the US Internal Revenue Code. There are two types of 529 plans: prepaid tuition plans and college savings plans. All fifty states and the District of Columbia sponsor at least one type of 529 plan.[32] There are also millions of financial aid dollars available in the form of scholarships and grants.

As leaders, we must take the time to understand the challenges our young black men face. Once we have information, we can begin to provide real customized solutions to help meet their financial needs. The United Negro College Fund's famous slogan "A mind is a terrible thing to waste" is a very important truth. Let's no longer allow the minds of young black men go to waste, due to an unwillingness

31 Anthony P. Carnevale, Nicole Smith, Jeff Strohl, RECOVERY: Job Growth And Education Requirements Through 2020;  Georgetown University Center On Education And The Workforce; Anthony P. Carnevale, Nicole Smith, Jeff Strohl;  pg. 15.

32 United States Securities and Exchange Commission, *Smart Saving for College*, NASD* http://www.sec. gov/investor/pubs/intro529.htm (Retrieved September 19, 2013).

to, as my dear mother would say, "bend our backs" and overturn the stones of college funding.

## If It Ain't Broke Don't Fix It

As we conclude this chapter we'd like to pose the initial question again: Are black boys brilliant or broken? If brilliant, they represent students who possess immeasurable intellect, talent, and skills that simply need to be honed and nurtured. If broken, how can they be restored or repaired? It is not appropriate to assume that something is malfunctioning if you don't honestly know how to operate it properly in the first place. In order to get maximum use out of something, you must first understand its function and the purpose for its creation. The word *broken* is defined as fractured, damaged, rejected, defeated, and weakened. There is a lot of talk about providing culturally relevant education. However, you cannot create culturally relevant pedagogy until you first understand the culture of those you are attempting to educate.

Maybe it's not black boys that are the problem. Could it be that those responsible for the education outside the home need to become more culturally relevant? You may not use the slang, but do you care enough to know what it means so that black boys will see you as one who is relevant? You may never wear sagging pants, but would you be willing to educate black boys on the importance of image and making strong first impressions? You may prefer *any* genre of music other than hip hop, but would you be willing to learn how the biographical stories of many of today's hip hop stars mirror the lives of the black male students you struggle to connect with on a daily basis? What if all nonblack educators understood that it is more likely for black males in the twenty-first century to be raised in single-parent homes? How might the future of the black family be different if we labored beginning in the primary years to affirm black boys in the education system rather than ostracizing them with labels, stereotypical attitudes, and pessimistic behavior? What if you saw the young black males in your classroom, your mentoring program, or on your sports team as the ones who could bring an end to the cycles of generational poverty in their family lineage? As we stated at the beginning of this book, you are either part of the problem or part of the solution. The honest answers to questions such as these will reveal whether you believe black boys are truly brilliant or irreparably broken.

# Action Steps

*What specific steps will you take to build or rebuild the will of a young black man in your sphere of influence who has given up on school?*

*If you are a parent, mentor, or extended family member of a young black man who is struggling academically, what will you do to collaborate with his teachers and the school system to help improve his academic achievement?*

*If you are a teacher or school administrator, what will you do to collaborate with parents, mentors, and extended family members to support the academic achievement of your black male students?*

# 8
# Don't Get Mad... Get Busy!

*In every day, there are 1,440 minutes. That means we have 1,440 daily
opportunities to make a positive impact.*
*- Les Brown*

For black men, attitude really is everything. We are often misjudged initially as a
result of our appearance. This is in part due to the media's stereotypical portrayal
of black men. Until we begin to speak, people have often formed a belief about
our ability to behave responsibly and communicate effectively. Therefore, it is
imperative for us to consider how our attitudes impact the ways in which we are
perceived. Let's consider the media's portrayal of the Seattle Seahawk's cornerback
Richard Sherman. Despite the fact that he is a Stanford University alum, has a high
football IQ, and plays his position with precision, he was labeled a "thug" after
his infamous interview with journalist Erin Andrews following the 2013 NFC
Championship game. Yes, he was excited, animated, loud, and perhaps angry, but
that interview was only a sound bite and in no way explains the whole of who he
is. Often black men are reduced to sound bites in the media, and judgments are
made about the entire black race, and black men in general, based on a twenty-
second interview. However, Sherman and many other intelligent black men are
passionate, and our passion can easily be misconstrued as anger.

As black men, we have to be tactful in how we express ourselves and our
passions so we avoid the label of "angry black man". If we are loud and speak with

passion and power, the assumption is typically negative. The result is that we often water down our expressions to avoid being labeled. In so doing, however, we miss the chance for the world to hear the best of us; they only get a watered-down, censored, and timid version of who we are. We have to teach black boys that being labeled should not prevent them from expressing themselves with passion. The world needs more of our passion and heartfelt expressiveness.

When my daughter was in kindergarten, I attended a function at her school. The parking lot bustled with excitement; face painting, basketball shooting contests, and plenty of other fun activities. The longest line was for the food vendor that had been contracted for the event. It seemed like almost everyone was in the line of hungry and sometimes impatient customers. I could tell that it was a bit stressful for the woman taking the orders.

I had already placed an order and was waiting for her to call my ticket when two black boys, who appeared to be between the ages of ten and twelve stepped up to the counter to place an order. I was impressed with how patiently they had waited for their turn. They politely placed an order using "Please," "May I," and all the other niceties we teach our children. I was proud, and I did not even know them.

In her busyness, the woman taking orders did not hear them and shouted, "I can't hear you!" Then she looked past them and continued calling out numbers. Both boys immediately put their heads down, and one of them hid under the booth window in an attempt to become invisible. They had done the right thing, but their voices had literally not been heard.

The woman happened to call my number next, but before I took my food, I looked at the boys, smiled at them, and told them that they had done an excellent job. I commended them for being patient, polite, and respectful, then I told them to look at the woman and speak up. Those boys had excellent attitudes and impeccable manners, and I wanted their voices to be heard.

How many times do those with attitude problems overshadow young black males with attitudes of promise? There were no press cameras at the vendor window highlighting the respectful and pleasant attitudes those boys displayed. If they had used profanity, threatened the woman, or robbed her, then they likely would have made the evening news. People would have watched and lamented about the tragic state of affairs and the dire condition of young black males. For every black man who has an attitude problem, there are many others with promising attitudes whose voices are not heard.

Much of my professional career has been in working with boys who have attitude problems and a callous disregard for others. The negative attention they have attracted has further tainted the image of the black male. As parents, mentors, counselors, and teachers working with black boys, it is important for us to focus our attention on the boys who demonstrate attitudes of promise. It hurt to see two polite and respectful young black males lose heart and confidence so quickly. I can only hope that my words inspired them. As black men, let's model how to speak up and speak out with passion, power, and conviction. We have boys who need to hear our voices and build their confidence so they can carry on and use those voices. If we are going to build strong black men with promising attitudes, they will need our voices to inspire and give courage to them.

As we seek to build strong black men we must communicate the following messages:

*Passion and anger are similar but not the same.* In many instances, the phrase "angry black man" could be replaced with the phrase "passionate black man." Passion and anger are similar, because they both represent strong emotion and energy. The distinctions are small, but clear. Let's take the Richard Sherman interview, for example. He showed passion when he talked about the rout and the play itself, but when he went after the San Francisco 49ers' Michael Crabtree, he displayed his anger. Anger left uncontrolled results in aggression and attacks on others that can be taken as having a negative attitude. I appreciated the fact that the media around Sherman also focused on the whole of who he is and did not leave us with just one interview.

*Uncontrolled anger can lead to destructive outcomes, but passion that is cultivated can lead to positive and powerful results.* We can cultivate passion by giving black boys an appropriate outlet to express themselves when they *are* angry or frustrated. It is important to note that anger is a normal and natural part of being human, but when, where, and how we express it makes all the difference. As young black men share their frustrations in a private context, we can help provide an appropriate interpretation and explain that there is nothing wrong with passion, but it must be controlled and focused. It is also important as we change the perception of who black males are. Often those mean scowls and discontented demeanors are often the result of displaced anger and other feelings that are not given the chance to go free. Instead, the black male you see who appears to have a bad attitude may just need to let off some steam but may not feel safe enough doing so.

*Having a positive attitude does not mean you are weak.* Smiling, greeting others, and behaving in a positive and respectful manner takes more strength than flying off the handle and "going ham" or "mean mugging" someone. It requires self-control and is a skill that black males must learn as we endeavor to be and to build strong black men.

*A positive attitude is a key to a positive future.* As we will discuss later in this chapter, your attitude can enhance your outlook and put you in a position to take advantage of the opportunities that present themselves. For example, the one thing that may separate you from others for a competitive job is your infectious positive attitude. Employers want people who bring positive energy to the workplace, and the way you present yourself in an interview can make a big difference.

## Your Greatest Asset and Greatest Liability

Your attitude is like a passport. It can take you a lot of places in this world. Whether those destinations are positive or negative is mostly up to you. How do you recognize a person who believes his attitude is his greatest asset? What type of life does a positive attitude produce?

## Positive Attitude

| Characteristics of a Positive Attitude | Common Results of a Positive Attitude |
| --- | --- |
| Motivated | Inspire yourself and others |
| Optimistic | Not discouraged by failure |
| Friendly | Attract positive people |
| Coachable | Success in school, sports, career, etc. |
| Respectful | People respect you |
| Generous | A life of fulfillment |

A positive attitude equals living a longer, healthier life; having closer personal relationships; being able to handle adversity; and learning from experiences. A negative attitude equals an untold number of negative things—even premature death.

People with positive attitudes smile frequently. They think good thoughts about themselves, and they think and speak positively about others. They also look for ways to make a positive impact on others and are on the receiving end of opportunities. People with good attitudes seem to make friends easier. The waiter with a good attitude will receive a larger tip than the waiter who is irritable and impatient. The athlete who is coachable will go further than the one who thinks he knows it all.

## Negative Attitude

| Characteristics of a Negative Attitude | Common Results of a Negative Attitude |
| --- | --- |
| Negative thinking | Overwhelmed by problems |
| Jealousy | Few quality relationships |
| Overeating | Poor physical health |
| Overly critical of self and others | Low self-esteem |
| Moody | Stress |
| Insecure | Abusive toward others |

## Attitude and Opportunity

As we mentioned, people with positive attitudes tend to seek and find opportunities. Sometimes opportunities come in the form of a test or challenge, and we have to demonstrate a positive attitude in order to pass or overcome. I have taken a lot of tests in my life. There were pop quizzes, open-book tests, driver's education tests, college entrance tests, swimming tests, midterm and final exams, vision tests, professional licensure exams, etc. When I was a student, I knew in advance when tests were going to take place; my teachers and professors told us the exact dates. They often went as far as providing a study guide so that we would know exactly what to review for the test. However, similar to the pop quiz, there are some tests that come unexpectedly. You don't receive any advance notice. Many of these tests have nothing to do with school or academics. These are tests given by Dr. Life.

Every day, in one way or another, we are tested in the areas of patience, courage, determination, endurance, understanding, integrity, wisdom, faith, and love. One test in particular that is very important for a young black man to anticipate is the test of opportunity. At some point in your life, you've probably heard someone say, "Opportunity is everywhere." We agree wholeheartedly with that statement. But not everyone has mastered the ability to recognize opportunities. They show up without calling first. They also do a good job of disguising themselves.

The prolific inventor Thomas Edison stated, "Opportunity is missed by most people because it is dressed in overalls and looks like work." What does this mean? It basically means that opportunities, especially good ones, will often look completely different than the picture we have in our mind. For example, an empty lot with overgrown grass is easy for most people to ignore. After all, there's nothing there but grass, right? Well, it depends on who's looking at the lot. Drive by that same piece of overgrown land with a successful real estate developer, ask him what he sees, and you may be surprised at his response. He may see a strip mall or a shopping center with numerous businesses and a paved parking lot filled with the cars of loyal customers, who will provide hundreds of thousands or even millions of dollars in annual revenue.

In other words, opportunity, similar to beauty, is in the eye of the beholder. So, if opportunity is everywhere, how does a young black man develop the ability to recognize it? We would suggest beginning to look for the opposite of what most people see. In order to recognize opportunity, begin to look for what's not there. The difference between the two perspectives of the vacant lot is vision. The first person saw only an empty lot with overgrown grass; the real estate developer saw a profitable shopping community. The developer did not deny that the "overalls" (the emptiness and the overgrown grass) were present. He just chose to look a little deeper to see the underlying opportunity to develop the land into something greater. In other words, the developer saw what was *not* there.

## Seeing the Big Picture

When I began driving legally with my learner's permit, I fondly recall my dad reminding me from the passenger seat to "look down the road." He wanted me to see the bigger picture while driving. It wasn't enough to merely pay attention to the car that was directly in front of me. Please don't misunderstand. There was certainly nothing wrong with my paying attention to the vehicle I was trailing. That was a good thing, but I was a new driver with limited vision. My father has always had a commercial driver's license, and he knew from his experience operating much larger vehicles that driving with limited vision could be fatal.

In chapter 4, we discussed the entertainment industry's impact on the way many young black men see themselves and their response to the "What do you want to be when you grow up?" question. Because of previous generations of intelligent and resilient black men and women, young black boys can become anything that their mind can achieve. The inauguration of Barack Obama in 2009 has proven that they can even be the president of the United States. Over the next few paragraphs, let's explore the importance of timing, preparation, location, and the ability to recognize and fulfill needs.

## Preparing for Opportunity

Timing is everything, and moving too quickly or too slowly on an opportunity can be detrimental to one's success. We can help young black men to recognize where they are now and assess why they may be receiving the opportunities they are being given. Each one is paramount to their future. Let them know that preparation is never lost time, and timing is everything. When the opportunity comes, they will be glad they were prepared.

I have seen the advantage of not moving too quickly and preparing for an opportunity firsthand. When my family relocated to a new state the summer of 2013, we left behind a home that we could not sell due to the low property values in our community. So we decided to put it on the market as a rental. It was in decent condition, but we spent the entire summer painting, laying down new flooring, fixing minor plumbing issues, and making sure all the general maintenance was completed. Since we were moving to a different state, we hired a company to handle the property management. Most of the companies that we interviewed told us that we were doing too much to fix up the property. They explained that most renters do not value a property very much, so there was no need to invest much time, energy, and money into fixing it up. We respected the advice, but we believed that renters would respect a house that was respectable. Once the house was ready, we put it on the market.

After the first thirty days we'd had numerous inquiries but no showings. The property manager advised that the rent we were asking for was too high.

We decided to keep the rent at the same rate, because a house next door to ours had a comparable rent. With only days' notice, our property manager resigned, and the property was left unattended until the contract expired about thirty days later. In the meantime, I worked to find a new property management company. I reviewed and interviewed dozens of companies with little success. Most were concerned that the rent was too high. However, we decided to stay firm with that rate. After weeks of continued searching, I found an organization that I considered hiring. The telephone interview was positive, and I told the property manager that I would discuss the details with my wife and follow up in a week.

Days later, I received a call from a real estate agent who had a client interested in renting the house. They were a couple who had been living in a one-bedroom condo in the uptown area of Charlotte, North Carolina. Rent in that area was easily double what we were asking. The couple saw our property as a deal, given that they were getting more space at half the cost.

As soon as I spoke with the real estate agent, I contacted and hired the property manager, and we created a contract. The couple signed the lease a few days later. We had done the legwork to prepare the property and to complete the painstaking process of hiring a new property manager. When the time was right, we were prepared to seize the opportunity when it presented itself.

## Location, Location, Location

When I was growing up, my favorite sport was basketball. Football was not too far behind. I remember my father's encouragement to give baseball a try, but my love for basketball and the aggressive schedule of annual AAU tournaments during the spring and summer was just too strong. I still love basketball and football, but as an adult I have also become a baseball fan. When I relocated to Georgia, my wife and I started to attend Atlanta Braves games regularly. I'm reminded of one particular game day when we were searching for parking close to Turner Field. As most fans do, we were following the signs for parking when we noticed a man waving a flag to get our attention. "You folks looking for a place to park?" the man asked as we waited for the line of cars in front of us to begin inching forward. "Uh … yes we are," I said, wondering if it was legit. He motioned with his hands for us to enter a small lot between two larger buildings.

The good news is that Turner Field was just a few blocks away. I had my doubts about parking there, but I noticed that his lot was half full, and the only activity in the area that would draw that many vehicles was the game. We decided to take our chances. After all, we figured we wouldn't be any worse off than the other car owners who had already parked there.

*Location directly affects the quantity and quality of opportunities you receive as well as the potential success of a career pursuit, idea, or business venture.*

After he finished guiding me to a vacant parking spot, I got out of the car, paid the parking fee, and being the inquisitive person that I am, asked him a few questions. "This lot must be pretty popular with the fans?" I asked, hoping to be convinced by his response. "Yeah, it does okay," he replied. Now, I didn't mean to seem nosy, but I was pretty sure that this older black man with a very easygoing personality and an extra large dose of humility knew something that I didn't know. "Okay?" I asked, trying to get him to elaborate. "It's only popular six months out of the year now, but it's not bad for an empty lot that I purchased back in the 1970s. It's paid for itself over and over again," he replied. At this point he had my full attention. I love to hear a good real estate investment story! "Do you ever go to the games?" I asked. "Not really. I usually just get here a few hours early on game day to open the lot, stay until the first couple of innings are over, and go home. Don't get me wrong, young man; I got nothing but love for the Braves! In a bad year they generate at least $30,000 for me during baseball season." He had a slight smile on his face.

Now, I knew why I needed to park in that lot. I needed a lesson on opportunity, and class was in session. He went on to explain that he bought the parcel of land back when the Braves were playing at the old Atlanta-Fulton County Stadium, decades before Turner Field was built. He purchased it based on the fact that this venue would consistently draw swarms of people in need of parking spaces for years to come. The 1996 Summer Olympics held in Atlanta and the construction of Turner Field were further confirmations of his wise decision. He mentioned that he had received tons of offers over the years to sell, but had always turned them down. Why? "Young man, I've already made more money than any of the individual offers were worth," he said. "It's not the prettiest lot I've ever seen, but this location has made it one of the most profitable."

Location is not to be ignored when evaluating opportunity. Depending on a young man's values, goals, and dreams, he may need to consider his location. A question to ask young men under your influence might be, "Does your current location help or hinder you from reaching your goal?" Location directly affects the quantity and quality of opportunities you receive as well as the potential success of a career pursuit, idea, or business venture. Expose young black men to visionaries so that they can be inspired by the stories and testimonials of those who have succeeded after seizing an opportunity.

## Filling a Need

An opportunist has the ability to find areas of need. Many inventions and companies exist today because someone was disturbed by a poor customer service experience or was required to perform a frustrating daily task. Or maybe they recognized that a product had some obvious or not-so-obvious limitations. They then made the product more affordable, portable, or user-friendly. Take just a few moments to think about the products that you use on a daily basis and then ask yourself, "What would my life be like without this product or service?" The products or services that we take for granted were once a tremendous opportunity that someone chose to capitalize on.

Opportunists ask questions like these:

- What's missing here?
- What would make peoples' lives easier?
- What is it that others are unwilling to do that I can do for them?
- What could save a lot of time?

If you make it a habit to develop the mindset of an opportunist and ask questions like these, you will inevitably arrive at a pretty good idea.

## Experience Is the Best Teacher

You live and you learn. People of all ages, ethnicities, and genders repeat variations of this statement. It sounds really good too. But is it true? It should be. However, even though we all make mistakes, very few of us pause afterward to take the time to reflect and process the who, what, when, where, and why that led to the mistake. Most of us just move along, say something clichéd like, "Well, you live and you learn," as we press the gas and accelerate rapidly toward our next mistake, only to repeat the cycle again! You will make mistakes. You don't have to learn from them. That is a choice. But in order to build strong black men, this must change.

> *You will make mistakes. You don't have to learn from them.*

## What About the I-Don't-Care Attitude?

One of my former client's had made great progress while he was in the youth development center. His treatment team recommended that he participate in a work program sponsored by an organization in his community. He had everything that he needed to succeed. He had therapy to help him continue to work on some of his behavioral and substance abuse problems, and unlike many young men leaving the facility, he had a *job*. Not only did the program include a job, but it also provided a uniform and even a bus pass so that he could get to and from work. His only task was to show up on Monday and pass a drug test. He was released on a Friday. He had been in a controlled environment for the past year, so I knew he had not used drugs. The next Monday morning, just three days after he was released, I received a call from the program coordinator, who informed me that he failed his drug test. That failed drug test disqualified him for the job. I wondered how this young man could let such a great opportunity to get off to a good start slip through his fingers. It is important to note that young men have to decide for themselves that they will make positive changes. I also remembered the adage "You can lead a horse to water, but you can't make him drink." We can create opportunities for our young men, but we can't make them recognize and embrace them.

Can you imagine a hot, dry day and a stream of fresh, cold water running endlessly at your feet? Even if you had to lead the horse to the water, you certainly wouldn't have to make a hot and thirsty horse drink once he got there. In some ways, our programming efforts to reach, support, and build our young black males at times has the opposite effect. We as parents, mentors, teachers, counselors, and supporters tend to want young black males to succeed more than they want to succeed for themselves. As a result, they are not thirsty, and they don't seem to care. We often make them too dependent on the program, and they do not learn to seize an opportunity. However, we do not believe the answer is to make our young men fend for themselves without any support or direction. The focus should be on developing an interdependent relationship where our young men have the opportunity to learn and grow on their own with our backing. However, we must make them thirsty and help them to seize the opportunities in front of them.

> We can create opportunities for our young men, but we can't make them recognize and embrace them.

One of my favorite movies of all time is *Remember the Titans*, starring Denzel Washington. The movie is based on the true story of a Virginia high school football team that brought black and white players together. They learned to play together, work together, and ultimately live out their lives together. One particular scene in the movie makes a strong point about the importance of giving our young men the opportunity to learn and grow. The head coach, played by Washington, was a tough, no-nonsense man who was tough on *all* the players. He refused to accept their excuses, and between the three-a-day practices, scarce water breaks, and early morning runs, he forged an attitude and spirit of determination and respect for the game and for each other.

The coach was particularly hard on one of the black players. He played on offense as a running back and had a problem with fumbling the ball. The first time it happened in practice, the young man blamed his blockers for not blocking well enough, and Washington made him run a mile. In a game, the young man missed a block, and Washington scolded him and took him out of the game. The assistant coach, played by Will Patton, was in charge of the defense. He went over to the young man and gave him the opportunity to play on defense. The young man did well, and the team won the game that night.

After the game Washington challenged Patton for taking it easy on the black players. He explained that he was trying to build character and to prepare *all* the young men to face life, and he explained that the world was not going to take it easy on the young black males on his team and neither should they. Both coaches represented the type of leadership that our young men need. Yes, young men need to be challenged to help prepare them for the tough and often harsh nature of the real world, but they also need to be encouraged and supported as they learn and grow.

Perhaps the young man in our program would have been better served if we had focused on helping him learn the soft skills of effective communication and on his knowledge about a particular industry or other career options. Even if he had passed his drug test and taken the job, he would have eventually had to find employment elsewhere. We could rest assured that he would not have been *given* his next job. He would likely have been competing with hundreds of others, including men and women who had families to feed.

## At the Car Wash

My last year in graduate school, my uncle got me a job working at a car wash. I savored the chance to work and to make extra money when home for the summer and during Christmas break. I got my first job when I was seventeen and kept it through my undergraduate years in college. I understood the value of hard work and had also learned to seize opportunities when they presented themselves. However, very little prepared me for what I experienced at the car wash.

I worked on the front end, which was very competitive. The front-end crew waited for the cars to come out of the wash and took them to a space on the lot where we hand-dried them, cleaned the doorjambs, cleaned the inside of the windows, and in some cases gave the car the "full treatment." The full treatment consisted of putting Armor All on the tires and the entire interior of the vehicle. The best tippers were usually the people who requested the full treatment. Some of the more experienced front-end workers could make well over one hundred dollars per day in tips alone. That particular car wash had a first-come, first-work policy. With the potential to make large sums of money, the drive to get on the clock first was strong. The business officially opened at eight o'clock in the morning. However, it was not uncommon for front-end workers to arrive as early as 7:00 am to ensure that they would be among the first to get on the clock. One day when I arrived at seven thirty, I did not get to start working until things got busier, which was nearly two hours later. I realized that if I wanted to work, I would have to get up earlier and get on the clock. No one seemed to care that I was the youngest employee or that my uncle was one of the best employees. My uncle's name and reputation got me the job, but neither my uncle nor anyone else was going to set my alarm clock and get me out of the bed in the morning.

Our young men do need fathers, uncles, mentors, and strong support in their lives, but they also need to learn to seize and to thrive in the opportunities that are provided for them. If we just give them a job, they may miss future opportunities. If we are going to *give* our young men anything, it should be the skills and ability to recognize and seize the opportunities that do come their way.

## Opportunities in Disguise

Not all opportunities look favorable in the beginning; in fact, some opportunities may look more like opposition or even oppression. I remember the pride and liberation I felt when I applied for my business license and started my practice not long after my resignation. I thought that if I was going to work hard, I might as well work hard for myself. The liberation of ownership impacted my thinking about value, business, and ultimately money. I had learned a valuable lesson, and one particular incident gave me the opportunity to share the lesson with a young black man.

I went to a locally owned service center to have my oil changed and met the owner in the front, where I selected my oil change package and paid him at the register. A few minutes after the technician had taken my car to the garage, he came out and asked me to come to the back. Once I was back in the garage, he explained that he had been working hard and was being paid very little for his efforts. He also explained that he was working there only long enough to finish school so he could get a better job. He went on to tell me that his dream was to open his own full-service shop. As encouraging as it was, I was a bit confused, because I was sure he did not call me to the back to tell me his dreams. After a few minutes, he said that he had a proposition for me. I am not certain whether or not he asked this of all his customers or just his black male customers. I thought maybe I looked like someone who he believed might take him up on his offer. He showed me that my air filter was dirty and needed to be replaced and then explained that they normally cost ten dollars, but he would give me a deal and charge me only five dollars. By the way, the owner had no idea that he was offering air filters at half-price. The young man explained that he would put the air filter on, and all I had to do was give *him* the five dollars. His reasoning was that he was doing all the work, and the owner was just sitting up front in the air-conditioning doing nothing.

As a new owner of a counseling practice, I knew that the owner had done a great deal to start his shop and that he likely did a whole lot more than just sit in the cool air. However, I knew telling the young man that would not translate because, in the moment, it was hot, and he was doing all of the work. I told him that I agreed that he was working hard and that I had no trouble giving him the five dollars, but as a tip. I also said that as a new business owner, I was also going to give the owner of the shop his ten dollars for the cost of the air filter, because he

> *Working hard means focusing on your work instead of the clock. It means giving a task your maximum effort, completing those tasks, and being attentive to details.*

took the risk to start the business and create jobs for others. I went on to point out to the young man that when he opens his shop, I am sure he would not want his employees making deals behind his back. The young man looked shocked, and when he finally began to speak, he said that he was going to remember what I told him. Of course I have no idea if he learned a lesson, but the point is that ownership is significant and our young men are capable of experiencing that.

Working hard for someone else may not feel like much of an opportunity, but we can help young men realize that while they are working, they should also be learning. The young man who changed my oil had the opportunity to learn firsthand the skills of the trade that he said he wanted to pursue. If he had the proper attitude, his paradigm would have shifted toward a realization that, based on his expressed vision, he was actually being paid *to learn*. We have to encourage young men to recognize and value opportunities that may not be obvious. Like diamonds in the ruff, opportunities are there and take a little work to discover. I don't know if he learned a lesson or if he eventually started his business, but here are two key insights from this story that are important for our young men to hear:

***Work with diligence and integrity, even if you don't like your job.*** Hard work and integrity are essential values for an entrepreneur to learn. If you aspire to own your own business, it is a good idea to start by working hard at your current job. Many people say they value hard work and that it is the key to success. But what does it actually mean to "work hard"? Working hard means focusing on your work instead of the clock. It means giving a task your maximum effort, completing those tasks, and being attentive to details. Even if that work is not your dream job, work hard stocking shelves, cleaning bathrooms, bagging groceries, or changing oil. The work ethic that you develop will serve you well once you have started your own business. It is also important to remember that integrity will keep you in business because being dishonest will catch up with you in time. Just ask individuals who have been convicted for not paying taxes or stealing money from their companies. Learn to do the right thing even when it does not seem to matter, because it will pay off.

***Owners look for opportunities to learn in every situation.*** The mind of a business owner looks at every situation as a chance to learn, and he always has his business aspirations in mind. For example, if you aspire to own a full-service auto repair and maintenance shop, and you are fortunate enough to work for someone who already owns a full-service shop, learn all you can. If you have a chance to interact with the owner, watch how he treats customers, addresses complaints, and handles the day-to-day business operations. Don't just stop at the end of your job description. Look for opportunities to learn about every aspect of the business. The reality is that, as a future owner, you will be responsible for your entire company.

## You Can Do Bad All by Yourself

We have talked about the positive outcomes of maintaining an attitude of promise and seizing opportunities. However, we have experienced black boys in our schools, churches, and communities who do have attitude problems. How do we address their attitudes and behavior to help unearth the promise that is buried underneath a mean mug, anger, and disruptive behavior? Two wrongs don't make a right. If a black male presents with an undesirable attitude in your class, group, after-school program, or home, it is crucial that you teach him how to present himself in a more positive light. We must remember to not allow the negative attitudes of young men with behavioral challenges to influence us as teachers, counselors, mentors, or caregivers.

One of the best gifts we can give is an example or a model of how to maintain a positive and productive attitude in any situation. I have witnessed and experienced repeated tests by young men who do their best to draw out a negative and combative reaction in others. Early in my career, I was facilitating a group in which one young man did everything in his power to draw me into a confrontation. He talked while I talked, got out of his seat, and tried to distract other students. There was a drink machine in the back of the room, and in one final desperate attempt to anger me, he climbed on it and tried to shake the drinks out.

It was clear that he wanted to anger and provoke me in the hope that I would dismiss him from the group. I did not get angry, and I did not remove him from the group. On the other hand, I didn't ignore him; I continued to invite him to participate in the group and to gain my attention in a positive manner. When he refused my questions, promptings, and proddings I went on with the group and interacted with the other students. I refused to get angry, and I refused to acknowledge his quest for negative attention. Once his peers saw that I was not going to get angry and was going to continue with the group regardless of what he did, they followed me.

I consistently invited his participation, and once he realized that I was not going to change my style, my approach, or my attitude toward him, he stopped and participated in the group. He had expended an enormous amount of energy trying to provoke me to kick him out. Not only had he not gotten a reaction from me, he had not even gotten a reaction from his peers.

In a subsequent one-on-one session, he explained that he did not want to be in the group and that he had decided that he was going to get me to kick him out. He said he was usually very easily able to get removed from classes and groups that he did not like. He told me that he could not believe that no matter what he did, I did not get mad and I did not kick him out. He said he asked himself, *"What is wrong with this guy?"* Nothing was *wrong*. And again, two wrongs don't make a right. I wanted to pull something more out of him and not feed into his plan, and he saw that presenting an adversarial attitude could no longer achieve his desired outcome.

> *It is important that we as men and leaders elevate young men to a level of respectfulness by our poise and positivity.*

I had to brave that storm, but he never tried me again, and he completed the group with no problems. Of course there are cases in which removal from a class or group setting becomes unavoidable and even necessary, but the key is to model a positive attitude in the process. As difficult as it was, I maintained my composure; I kept an even tone of voice, made eye contact, listened to other students, smiled, and treated the wayward student with respect. My demonstration was for the other students to see how to maintain a positive disposition in a tough situation. The other students took their cues from me. They followed my example, and the overall energy in the room remained positive.

I commend all of those willing to work with young people within the educational, juvenile justice, or human services systems. I am learning that many of the young men who end up in our systems have a need to see that having a pleasant demeanor can take them further than the mean mug and angry scowl that some of our young men have grown accustomed to wearing on their faces. They likely have had many models for how to fly off the handle, cuss, fuss, and fight. If we as professionals meet them at that level, we are in a lose-lose situation, and we as professionals and adults have a lot more to lose. It is important that we as men and leaders elevate young men to a level of respectfulness by our poise and positivity. We must not allow negativity to coax us into a battle that teaches them that they can get what they want through their oppositional and defiant behavior. Sometimes, despite our best efforts, our young men may still insist on carrying around a disposition of negativity. When this happens, let's make sure that they do not carry us or others down with them; let's make sure they are doing bad all by themselves.

## Don't F— the Police

Any discussion about the importance of attitude and its role in building strong black men in the twenty-first century has to include instructions on how to relate to the police. It is common for a black man to have had some type of negative or at least questionable experience with a police officer. A Gallup poll taken in July 2013 revealed that 24 percent of black males surveyed reported that they had experienced some type of mistreatment by police within a thirty-day period. That is almost a quarter, and it is even more alarming because it took into account only a thirty-day period. What would the survey have revealed if eighteen- to twenty-four-year-olds were asked the same question expanded to include their lifetime?[33]

Even well-educated, prominent black men can be recipients of questionable police practices. Take Harvard professor Henry Louis Gates, for example. He was

---

33 Frank Newport, In U.S., 24% of Young Black Men Say Police Dealings Unfair, http://www.gallup.com/poll/163523/one-four-young-black-men-say-police-dealings-unfair.aspx (Retrieved July 15, 2014).

arrested for disorderly conduct after police were called to his home because he was suspected of burglary. He was trying to get into his own house after he returned to his home to find the door jammed. The arrest ignited a national outrage and provoked discussions of race, power, and police profiling. Perhaps both Gates and the Sgt. James Crowley were at fault, but the potential for a black man to be met with suspicion and fear do not halt even in the face of education, prestige and class.

It is clear that in both the past and the present, black men have not had the most positive experiences in their interactions with police. Of course, it is arguable that the Gallup poll is a compilation of the perceptions of people's personal experiences and that those in a larger audience may not have considered the police behavior to be questionable. Or they may have been able to offer explanations and even justifications for the actions of the police. However, perception is reality, especially in an era when black male teens can be gunned down due to their clothes, their music, or because someone is afraid that they *may* be doing something wrong.

I too have experienced interactions with police that left me questioning their motives and my own safety. I was sitting parked in my 1978 Ford Pinto on a warm spring day. I had just left church and was reflecting on the sermon when a police car approached me. The car passed, and moments later it turned around and pulled up behind me with lights flashing. My mind raced to figure what could have caused the police to approach my parked car. There was no possibility of speeding, an improper lane change or failure to use my turn signal; and my tags were up-to-date. My mind raced for a way to explain this apparent unprovoked stop, but I was at an utter loss. An array of emotions flooded my mind; anger, fear, and confusion were the most prominent. I had done nothing wrong and had nothing to hide. The funny part was that I had just left church, with my Bible open, and wearing my Sunday best. What was it about me that looked so suspicious?

After a few minutes, I suppose the time that it took to run my plates; the policeman emerged from his car and approached me. My window was already rolled down, and I had my license and registration ready to present to him. By the time he reached my car window, another police car had pulled up behind me. The fact that two officers were now behind me increased my level of fear and confusion. I wondered why one officer would pull up behind me as I was simply minding my own business. However, the presence of the second caused me to feel a little threatened and intimidated. The first officer did not ask for my license and registration. He asked me what I was doing and why I was sitting in the car. I explained that the sermon at church inspired me and I wanted to reflect on what the pastor said. My senses grew even more heighted when he did not ask for my license and registration. It felt very unprofessional and it left me unsettled. As he continued to question why I was sitting in my car, my discomfort increased and I began to feel violated. It made me feel that somehow he was questioning my right to sit in my own car and mind my own business on a peaceful Sunday afternoon. What was wrong with that? To this day, I have no idea why they approached me, because they never offered me an explanation.

Despite my emotions of fear, and eventually anger, I maintained my composure. My mother did not teach me the formal rules of engagement when pulled over by a police officer, but she did teach me manners, and you better believe I used every "Yes sir" and "No sir" I could muster. I gave them no reason to fear me or view me as a threat. Even though I fought to avoid it, I could not chase away the thought that the only reason they were at my window was because I was black. Whether that was true or not could be debated, but I made sure not to give him or his colleague any *legitimate* reason to ticket or arrest me.

By chance I happened to glance at his name badge and noticed that his last name was very familiar. It took seconds for me to place the name. His wife was the vice president of the organization where I was completing my internship. She had mentioned him and his police work frequently. She had even shown me pictures of him and their family, including their dog.

He had been asking me questions, which by law, I did not have to answer. Once I realized that he was my Vice President's husband, I asked about her by name, their children, and even their dog. I explained that I was completing my internship at her organization and that she spoke of him often. The look on his face was one of astonishment mingled with shame. With haste he said, "Well, I just wanted to check to make sure everything was okay." Then he left, with his partner not far behind.

For black men, being pulled over by the police is often a reality, and it is possible that the only reason the officer or officers pulled you over is because of your race. Again, that is debatable. However, you have to make sure that you give the officer no reason to arrest or charge you. Make sure you are not the one in the wrong, and if you are in the wrong, take responsibility and show respect to the officer. You cannot control whether or not the police stop you, but you can control your attitude toward them.

A bigger concern for our young men is what unprovoked stops by the police do to our psyche. I am disturbed by the number of young men who have either an unhealthy fear of the police or an "f— the police" attitude. We were not made to live in fear or with persistent resentment. Both fear and resentment have lingering consequences that trickle into all aspects of our lives. I have worked with and witnessed many young black men who appear to be mad at the world. They carry a chip on their shoulders, and the way they present themselves is adversarial; they just dare people to do or say anything to give them an excuse to go off. I have met others who fear the police and do not trust them. They avoid the police in fear that they will be stopped for something, and in so doing they make themselves look guilty even when they are not. A strong black man has no need to fear or to f— the police.

As you advise young men, in how they interact with police, remember these important tips:
- Yes, there are bad police officers, but most truly do want to protect and serve.
- They have loved ones.

- They want to go home safely after a day's work.
- They would rather not have an ugly confrontation with you.
- Most will treat you with respect, especially when you treat them with respect.

But also remember to tell them:
- They are human.
- They make mistakes.
- They work in a difficult profession.
- They are not your enemy and are there to protect and serve you as well as others.
- They cannot charge you if you are doing nothing illegal.
- They don't want your fear, and they don't deserve your resentment and disrespect.
- Don't f— the police.

## Don't Get Mad, Get Busy

You may feel the police, your teachers, your parents, or your boss are not treating you fairly. You may expect others to give you a break or cut you some slack. I have witnessed many young men who have worked to improve their behavior and adopt a more positive attitude and then expect you to celebrate and give them the royal treatment; but they are just doing what they are supposed to do in the first place. Yes, we should celebrate our young men when they are making improvements, but we have to remind them that society expects them to function in a positive and productive manner. They should not expect a red-carpet reception every time they stay out of trouble or do well on a class assignment.

As a former New York City resident, I've had my share of entertaining rides on the subway going back and forth among the boroughs of Brooklyn, Queens, the Bronx, and Manhattan. I refer to these public transportation excursions as exciting because, quite frankly, you just never know what you might see! On many occasions I have witnessed black men, both young and old, make presentations of athletic, musical, rhythmic, and oratorical excellence.

During one of the frequent train stops, a young black man who appeared to be in his late teens or early twenties boarded the train and immediately began to inform the passengers of his intentions. His goal was to sell packs of M&M's that were priced somewhere between fifty cents and a dollar. Usually the presenter says it is for some heart-tugging charitable cause, but this young man had no such cause. He merely stated that he was a young black man who was "trying to do something positive" with his time rather than participating in crime. That's it. Not only was his sales pitch underwhelming, but his tone of voice, which was already aggressive, became very angry the closer we got to the next stop on the

> *"Don't waste energy getting mad when you can take the same energy and get busy learning and developing your skills so you can achieve success."*

train. He was obviously frustrated because there were very few people willing to purchase M&M's based on his presentation. However, it was not just his tone of voice that was repelling potential customers. It was the fact that he thought he was entitled to our money simply because he presented himself as a law-abiding black man. There are many reasons this is problematic, the least of which is that you don't typically receive rewards for doing what you are supposed to do. Again, there was nothing substantial about his presentation. As a matter of fact, all the passengers on the train were doing the same thing he was attempting to do at that moment: obey the law. Why he thought that should be enough for us to empty our wallets in generosity was cause for concern.

When the train reached its next stop, he departed, angrily proclaiming that *we* should be ashamed of ourselves due to our unwillingness to "help a brother out." This man demonstrated at least two attitude problems. First, he had an attitude that suggested that because he was black, he was more likely to engage in nefarious activity, and thus for him to obey the law was an exceptional accomplishment. Second, even if he wanted complete strangers to support his cause, the angry tone of entitlement he used was a complete turnoff. I certainly would have been more inclined to give money to a person that was nice and humble. Besides, being black doesn't make it harder to obey the law.

It would be easy to categorize that young man on the subway as part of the bad-attitude group. But in some ways he was exercising some initiative and may have benefited from some basic communication skills. If he would have been willing to learn, his sales pitch could have been transformed into something much more passionate and compelling. He was a great example of an angry young man with a wealth of passion waiting for the guidance and direction to harness it into something beautiful. In his mind, helping a brother out may have meant purchasing all the candy, but the real help he needed was skills so that he could sell more candy and from there maybe cars, computers, or stocks. To our fellow black males who are angry and feel that they are entitled to something we say, "Don't waste energy getting mad when you can take the same energy and get busy learning and developing your skills so you can achieve success."

## There's Power in Your Thoughts

How do you respond to adversity? What drives you? Consider the following scenario. Thomas is a black male who grew up in a single-parent home without his father. He has never met his father and wouldn't recognize him if the two of them were standing in the same room. Thomas believes he has little value because his father did not take the time to show love and affection to him, provide for him, and teach him how to be a man. Instead of living a healthy, productive life, he chooses to allow the anger, insecurity, and confusion stemming from the void created by his father to drive his life. This causes Thomas to have a fear of commitment, especially when it comes to relationships. Thomas learned by watching his father's bad example that it's okay to be uncommitted. He also thinks that he will never be a good father because, after all, he didn't have his own father's approach to glean from. Thomas lashes out at others in anger when things don't go his way. He believes that things don't go his way because he's not worthy of success. He doesn't know the value of women, so he chooses to use them as sexual objects. As a result, Thomas has fathered several children outside of marriage. He is not committed to the children's mother, so he feels no obligation to commit to them. Thomas thus repeats the cycle all over again. He justifies it because, after all, the children will be better off without him, because he doesn't know how to be a father anyway. All of this stems from a negative mental attitude.

Now let's consider the impact of a positive mental attitude in the exact set of circumstances above. Thomas has never met his father but has been fortunate to have strong black male influence in the form of a supportive grandfather, uncles, black male teachers, mentors, and athletic coaches. Instead of being bitter and giving the cold shoulder to these men because they are not his father, he recognizes these relationships as opportunities to learn all he can about manhood. Rather than allowing his biological father's absence, which is completely out of his control, to influence him negatively, he decides to practice being grateful for every positive male influence he has in his life. Thomas has learned how to be a man by observing and listening to words of wisdom from these strong black men. Unlike his father, he decides he will be faithful when engaging in an intimate relationship with a female, because he wants to experience the joy of a committed relationship. He vows to be the type of father to his future children that the positive, strong black male influences in his life have encouraged him to be, because he wants to create a legacy of engaged fatherhood in his family.

> *You are where you are today because of the attitude and beliefs you held over the last five years. In five more years, you will be where your current attitude is taking you.*

## Your Attitude Shapes Your Future

Ask yourself this question: "Is my present attitude taking me closer to or further away from the manifestation of my desired future?" You are where you are today because of the attitude and beliefs you held over the last five years. In five more years, you will be where your current attitude is taking you. Our thoughts influence both our attitudes and our behaviors. For example, if you are overly critical of yourself and guided by thoughts of self-doubt and insecurity, you won't be able to muster up the motivation to study to get better grades in school or to start that business that you have been hoping to launch for years now.

A negative attitude will keep you discouraged and feeling incapable of making progress. It will also repel the very people that you will need to accomplish the various goals and dreams that you set for yourself. Remember this: nothing in this world has ever been done or will ever be done without the efforts and interaction of people. People are imperfect; we all make mistakes. If you are unwilling to work, communicate, and interact peaceably with other people, you can expect to have a miserable life. A positive attitude can cause you to overcome what, in many cases, seems impossible.

# Action Steps

*What can you do to positively shape the attitudes of black boys with attitude problems?*

*How can you teach young black men to see and seize opportunities?*

# Epilogue

Thank you for your commitment to read this book! The work of building strong black men is a lifelong endeavor that passes from one generation to another. When we were children our elders told us that we were the future. We benefited from the influence of older and wiser individuals who helped to mold and shape us into the men we are today. Now as elders, we recognize that offering the same guidance to the next generation of young men is now our responsibility. In the twenty-first century young black males face obstacles that may seem insurmountable. For some lying in the balance, our efforts will be the difference between life or death, freedom or incarceration, and fatherhood or the continued generational impact of fatherlessness. Every generation has experienced difficulty and struggle. However, throughout history we have been given countless examples for how to overcome adversity.

So, where do we go from here? Forward. From the initial conception of the idea for this book, it has been our collective goal to provide a foundational blueprint for the successful building of young black men. It is our aim to help them to be the imitable leaders, husbands, fathers, and mentors that they were designed to be. The work to build strong black men is massive, but possible. The opportunities are plenteous, but too much for any individual to attempt to conquer alone. It will take a concerted effort on the part of all those involved. Parents, extended family members, teachers, mentors, coaches and counselors have roles to play in the process. The young black males of today are our future, and they are worth the effort that it will take. We cannot afford to wait until an incident involving the senseless loss of life of another black male plays out on national television before we decide to take action. We must not stand back and complain about the plight of black males when we can use the same energy to create positive change. It is only when we take personal ownership of the problems facing the black male community that we can begin to see statistics reversed and mindsets changed.

In order for black lives to matter to others, they must first matter to *us*! We must be diligent to demonstrate this *before* the public demonstrations of marching, protesting, and rioting. When they truly matter to us, solutions such as the ones provided throughout this book, will be implemented with fervor and such regularity that we will no longer look to the media to inform us about the status of black men. We will already know their status because our sleeves are rolled up and our hands calloused from the work of upholding the legacy passed down from previous generations. We encourage you as the reader to take the ideas, examples, and energy from this book and use them as a source of inspiration and conviction as you fight to improve the lives of black men around the world. There has never been a better time to become dedicated and committed to this work, and it is more necessary now than ever before.

# Acknowledgements

Nothing worth doing is easy and this endeavor has been worth the time, energy, late nights and early mornings necessary to complete. Nor is any great work birthed without support. This project did not begin in 2012 when we embarked on this journey; it began years earlier when my mother instilled the values that shaped me into the man I am today. Thank you for leading me by example and showing me constant love and support. I am thankful for my sister whose quiet strength inspires me. You always remember the little things that make a big difference. I am grateful for my maternal grandparents, aunts, cousins and uncles who supported my mother as a single parent. I am blessed to have a wife who is always honest and tells me what I need to hear not just what I want to hear. Thank you for helping me to become a better man. It is my privilege and honor to raise three wonderful children who I pray will carry on the legacy I am building. Finally, to Zack Reynolds, Jr., my co-author, brother and friend, we did it! I am proud that we completed this work, and I anticipate the future as we labor to leave a legacy of strong black men.

**Jeremiah Hopes**

It has taken a lifetime to gather the experiences and thoughts shared within the pages of this book and I would like to acknowledge those essential to my evolution into manhood. First, I am grateful to God for the gifts that He has given and for giving us the ability and desire to complete this work. To my father, thank you for modeling my entire life what it truly means to be a strong, black man. Your presence and the blueprint you've provided have demystified many of the challenges related to navigating manhood. To my mother, thank you for your love, words of wisdom, and guidance that have helped shaped my desire to communicate messages of hope to others. To my sister, you are an inspiration and a great example of how to selflessly give to others. I am honored to be your brother. I am grateful for the legacy of my paternal and maternal grandparents, my extended family, and all the great examples of strong men within who have helped to provide proper perspective. To my beautiful daughter Zeal, I am so grateful to call you my little girl and for how your presence keeps me accountable to the messages written on the pages of this book. To my wife Christal, thank you for sharing your life and love with me. You have been there every step of the way, encouraging, critiquing, and confirming. I am grateful for your candor and willingness to sacrifice as I seek to fulfill my purpose in life. You make me better. Finally, to Jeremiah Hopes, thank you for actively modeling the definitions of friend, brother, mentor, counselor, and business partner. I'm proud that we can now officially add "co-author" to the growing list of experiences shared. Here's to the future!

**Zack Reynolds, Jr.**

# About The Authors

Though the initial conversation that led to the writing of this book occurred in March 2012, the story that allowed this work to come to fruition actually began many years earlier in Greensboro, NC. It is a story where the pages of friendship and destiny were written before the authors met and that continuously speaks to the power of connection and authentic friendship. The University of North Carolina at Greensboro would provide the setting where the two young black men would actually meet, but under very unique circumstances. Jeremiah was a graduate student, also serving as a resident director for the academic year. Zack was an incoming freshman with intentions to transfer to the University of North Carolina at Chapel Hill after completing a year of study. Throughout the year, the two became friends and, though ultimately deciding to go separate ways to complete their respective college studies, committed to stay in touch. A mentor once shared with Zack that everyone you meet in life comes into your life for a reason, a season, or a lifetime. The power of relationship, destiny, and purpose has the ability to supersede the plans of mere mortals. These young men never would have imagined that when they introduced themselves on that scorching summer day in August that years later they would eventually become co-authors. Over the years, as they have grown personally, spiritually, and professionally as black men, they have developed a unity that speaks more to brotherhood rather than friendship. Though both men could have written a book of this subject matter individually based on their experience, they decided to co-author intentionally. *Facing Our Future: Building Strong Black Men In The Twenty-First Century* represents the merger of their individual and professional backgrounds as they have labored fervently in their local communities to improve the lives of young black men via the fields of education, counseling, and mentoring.

# AUTHOR BIOGRAPHIES

## Jeremiah Hopes

Jeremiah Hopes is a professional counselor, keynote speaker, and professional trainer. He speaks across the country on topics including ADHD, anger, addictions, diversity and innovative clinical approaches.

In 2005, he founded The Center of Hopes™ a counseling, speaking, and training organization committed to the prevention of juvenile delinquency. Jeremiah has learned that keeping youth off the path to delinquency is a collective effort. Therefore, he offers cutting-edge training to parents, professionals, and other partners who work directly or indirectly with youth.

## Zack Reynolds, Jr.

Zack Reynolds, Jr. is an alumnus of the University of North Carolina at Chapel Hill and the Coaching and Positive Psychology Institute. A dynamic educator, life coach, and motivational speaker, he specializes in helping others maximize their personal and professional potential.

After years of working with underserved youth in rural and urban communities, his influence began transcending the classroom. He is the co-founder of Minorities Achieving Postsecondary Success, Inc. (MAPS), a college access and success organization. Also a talented musician and entertainment professional, Zack has performed and consulted extensively with various recording artists, songwriters, and producers across the United States.

# Notes

# Notes

# Notes

# Notes

# Notes